AN ANNOTATED BIBLIOGRAPHY OF MULTI-CULTURAL LITERATURE AND RELATED ACTIVITIES FOR CHILDREN THREE TO TEN YEARS

An Annotated Bibliography of Multi-Cultural Literature and Related Activities for Children Three to Ten Years

Guda Gayle-Evans

Mellen Studies in Children's Literature
Volume 6

The Edwin Mellen Press
Lewiston•Queenston•Lampeter

Library of Congress Cataloging-in-Publication Data

Gayle-Evans, Guda.
   An annotated bibliography of multi-cultural literature and related activities for
children three to ten years / Guda Gayle-Evans.
         p. cm. -- (Mellen studies in children's literature ; v. 6)
      Includes [bibliographical references] and index.
      ISBN 0-7734-6474-3
      1. Pluralism (Social sciences)--United States--Juvenile literature--Bibliography. 2.
Pluralism (Social sciences)--Juvenile literature--Bibliography. 3. Ethnology--United
States--Juvenile literature--Bibliography. 4. Ethnology--Juvenile literature--Bibliography.
5. Children's literature, American--Bibliography. 6. Children's literature--Bibliography. 7.
Pluralism (Social sciences) in literature--Bibliography. 8. Ethnology in
literature--Bibliography. 9. Minorities in literature--Bibliography. 10. Children--Books and
reading--United States--Bibliography I. Title. II. Series.

   Z1361.E4G39   2004
   [E184.A1]
   016.3058'00973--dc22
                                                                    2004040202

This is volume 6 in the continuing series
Mellen Studies in Children's Literature
Volume 6 ISBN 0-7734-6474-3
MSCL Series ISBN 0-7734-7322-X

A CIP catalog record for this book is available from the British Library.

Front cover: Artwork by Valencia Sin-Clare (California, USA)

Copyright © 2004   Guda Gayle-Evans

            The Edwin Mellen Press   The Edwin Mellen Press
                   Box 450   Box 67
            Lewiston, New York   Queenston, Ontario
            USA 14092-0450   CANADA L0S 1L0

                        The Edwin Mellen Press, Ltd.
                        Lampeter, Ceredigion, Wales
                        UNITED KINGDOM SA48 8LT

                     Printed in the United States of America

Dedicated to the memory of my sister Kathleen (Gayle) Williams
who made the combination of summer and reading such a delightful memory

Table of Contents

Preface

America has long been recognized as a country of immigrants, but at no time has the influx of immigrants been greater than it has been over the past three decades. Unlike during the early days of immigration when most of the immigrants were from Europe, immigrants today are from all parts of the world. The largest numbers are from Europe and Asia and the Hispanic countries. The 1990 Census Bureau showed that about twenty million of the nation's total population were foreign born. In addition to immigrants and their descendants there are the American Indians and African Americans. This *potpourri* of cultures make for an exciting time to explore and learn more about peoples of differing values and lifestyles. Children are sometimes overlooked when the importance of diversity training and multicultural experiences are discussed. Children, like adults, also are curious about the different cultural groups they encounter in their schools. They too ask questions about the foods, clothing, language and lifestyles of their classmates.

Age appropriate books provide one of the most enjoyable and explicit means of providing information about different cultures. They help children's under-standing of the ways cultures are alike and instances in which they differ. These very books, when integrated into the curriculum to teach concepts in the different content areas, allow for the mainstreaming of multiculturalism rather than the perception of it being a separate area of study. Readers will also become aware of cultural difference not as the perceived anomaly but as a phenomenon that is to be embraced.

Juxtaposed on the ethnic cultures are the micro-cultures such as age, gender exceptionality, language, religion and social class. This cultural *Kaleidoscope* has been captured in a unique annotated list of over three hundred books compiled by the author. The list is extensive not only in number but in its usefulness to achieve the goals set out by the author. The multicultural topics are extensive. They include clothing, travel, intergenerational relationships, food, celebrations, folktales and moral issues such as good over evil.

In addition to the main listing the various appendices are particularly useful. For example, Appendix A has been carefully designed to give the teacher a list relating to content areas such as Art, Mathematics and the Social Sciences. Appendix B contains suggested activities and Appendix C has a listing related to the micro-cultures.

This annotated bibliography is extremely remarkable in the many utilitarian possibilities. Teachers interested in expanding multicultural education across content areas could not ask for a better source for information. The wide classification that incorporates cultures and micro-cultures make this volume invaluable. The activities respond to the concerns of teachers of young children: they are interesting, enjoyable and very informative. They also make a good addition to any curriculum program.

Although the book's target population is mostly teachers, parents will also find this list very helpful as they try to answer their children's questions about different cultural groups. The nature of the list will also allow parents and teachers to decide what books they want to read to children, what lesson they want the children to grasp from the stories and what activities they may want the children to experience. The stories chosen will also provide opportunities for good parent-child interaction time that is fun and informative and that can also be emotionally rewarding for both the adult and the child.

I commend the author on this one of a kind masterpiece.

Lena Hall
Nova Southeastern University

Foreword

Children become aware of physical differences at a very early age. Early positive exposure to differences whether physical, social, emotional or cognitive will help to diminish viewing any form of difference in a negative way. One very important medium for providing this experience is through multicultural books. Multicultural books allow children to enter the world of reality and imagination while allowing them to gain a different perspective on people and places that may be different. Multicultural books take children to a world to which they may not otherwise be exposed, a world with which many children may not be familiar. However, whether it is a world of reality or a world of fantasy, it will most likely be a world of fun.

Interest in this project was based on a desire to become familiar with multicultural children's books. Later, as I worked with preservice teachers and also as a presenter at local, regional and international conferences, I listened to teachers' and students' concerns as to when and how to use multicultural books. My interest grew as I realized there is a great need for a project such as this. This project is an attempt to provide teachers with a list of multicultural children's books and some activities that can be included in the early childhood classroom.

I have read and enjoyed the variety of books included in this annotated bibliography. However, I urge teachers and parents to also read the books, as they would normally do, before presenting them to children. In choosing books, it is important to remember that the interest of the teacher or parent, as well as the children, is important.

In the annotated listing, I have indicated stories which took place long ago. I urge parents and teachers to pay particular attention to this factor. Stereotypes are reinforced by children confusing past cultures with those of the present. When sharing books about the past, especially as related to Asian and Indigenous Peoples, it is vitally important to remember that members of these cultures are our contemporaries. Although some members may choose to remain close to their traditional ways, children should be made aware that members of these groups live among us and, although their cultures are unique, they enjoy many of the same things that we do.

The Annotated listing contains books that I believe will be of interest to children ages three to ten years or older. However, these ages are meant to be used only as a guideline. The activities, in Appendix B, are also meant to interest children ages three to ten years old. However, younger children may be interested in some activities meant for older children. I have also included with the activities in Appendix B, some books from the listing that I believe will be supported by the activities. Once again, these are only meant as suggestions. For convenience, the activities are listed according to content areas and in each content area the books are listed in alphabetical order by the title of the first book, where there are multiple listings. For each activity in Appendix B I have included an age level as well as skills that can be gained or developed from each activity. Again, these are only suggestions.

It is important for children to be aware that although there are many people around the world who are different from us in many ways, we are alike in many more ways. To that extent, I have included after each activity or each group of like activities, a section titled: *Suggestion to Broaden Cultural Awareness*. In each of these sections I have provided ways, related to the activity or activities, in which I believe parents and teachers can extend children's knowledge about other cultures.

For convenience I have included Appendix C. In this section the annotated books are listed under categories of microcultures such as age, ethnicity, exceptionality, gender, language, race, religion and social class. These are microcultures that are most likely to impact the curriculum. However, it should be noted that many of the books, in the annotated listing as well as Appendix C, may be used in several categories with any appropriate age group. The categories provided are based solely on my preference.

It should also be noted that being from a different culture and having lived in different cultures, my interpretation of multiculturalism is quite broad. I have, therefore, included books that may not typically be considered multicultural. For example, the books *Are You My Mother?* (Eastman, 1963), *Stellaluna* (Cannon, 1993), *Blueberries for Sal* (McCloskey, 1948) and *The Very Hungry Caterpillar* (Carle,1987), would not typically be considered multicultural books. However, *Are You My Mother*, *Blueberries for Sal*, and *Stellaluna* can be used when teachers discuss families and family dynamics. *Blueberries for Sal* and *The Very Hungry Caterpillar* will expose children from a different region or economic level in the United States or children from a different culture, to foods to which they may not necessarily be familiar. For example, the caterpillar eats foods indigenous to the region in which it lives. Also, the word "plum" is used to apply to a variety of fruits depending on area of the United States and also the country or culture. This is also true of the word "cherry". Many children will enjoy researching these facts.

I have included a wide variety of books from various cultures. I have included old favorites such as *Did You Carry the Flag Today, Charlie?* (Caudhill, 1966) and *How the Rhinoceros Got His Skin* (Kipling, 1988). I have also included some more recent stories. The list of books is extensive but by no means exhaustive. I believe that the ways in which teachers and parents can extend the stories are almost unlimited. The creativity of the teacher or parent is the only limit. I had a great deal of fun reading the stories and hope that teachers, parents and children will also enjoy the books which I selected.

Guda Gayle-Evans, Ph.D.
St. Petersburg, Florida

Acknowledgments

I am deeply indebted to all who supported me throughout this project especially Noga Gayle, Venus McGregor-Lowe and Lena Hall. Thanks so much for never being too busy to listen. Lena, thanks for feeling free enough to tell me "It's time." Thanks to friends Gloria Maccow and Larry Johnson. Like Lena and Noga you allowed me to "bounce ideas off you." I will be forever grateful. Thanks to my colleagues at the University of South Florida St. Petersburg. Your support throughout the process will always be remembered.

Thanks to the memory of my brother Bertram Gayle. You have taught me more in the past two years than you will ever know. Last, but certainly not least, thanks to the memory of my parents, Charles and Leanora Gayle. After all these years you still continue to amaze me. Thank you both so much for everything you gave me.

Introduction

Young children are innately curious. They naturally seek to find out about their environment and their world. In the early years, they use their senses - seeing, listening, smelling, feeling and tasting to gain knowledge. The more they are able to interact with people and objects, the more likely it is that they will gain the needed knowledge. They build upon prior knowledge, making connections with what they already know through the process of assimilation and accommodation (Piaget & Inhelder, 1969). We also know that children learn from the general to the specific (Comenius, 1967). They will, therefore, understand the concept animal before they can differentiate between dog, cat or squirrel. To help children build on and reconstruct prior knowledge, a variety of opportunities must be provided for them to explore. This is also applicable when we think of culture.

Culture is the way we think, feel and behave as a society (Chinoy & Hewitt, 1975; Gollnick & Chinn, 2002). Everyone is born into a culture. Although we may think one's culture is intrinsic, culture is actually learned (Chinoy & Hewitt, 1975; Gollnick & Chinn, 2002). What we learn within our culture is taught, modeled and reinforced. Young children do have a difficult time learning about their culturally defined world. It is part of a process of development. Therefore, if young children are outside the culture, it is likely to be even more difficult for them to learn about the new culture.

Children need to learn that there are people who speak differently, dress differently and even wear different types of clothing (whether it is based on religion or climatic conditions) than they do. Teachers, therefore, need to include multiculturalism in as natural a way, as possible, in the classroom. This means that as children learn about people in general, they also learn specifically about people who may not look, speak or dress the way they do. Young children also gain a different perspective as they learn how people from different cultures are likely to see things in a different way. Gaining perspective may be especially difficult because we know that children younger than eight years old tend to be egocentric (Piaget & Inhelder, 1969).

How Does Culture Manifest Itself?

Culture is manifested in many ways. Each culture has its definition of what is valued and, therefore, manifestation takes many forms. However, the most basic forms of manifestation may include the clothing that is worn, food that is eaten, how words are spoken and ways in which behaviors are exhibited. Manifestation of culture also includes values that members of that culture view as important (Chinoy & Hewitt, 1975; Gollnick & Chinn, 2002).

What Is Multicultural Education?

Since the nineteen seventies several definitions have been offered for multicultural education. According to Gollnick and Chinn (2000), "education that is multicultural provides an environment that values diversity and portrays it positively." The United States is moving from an agrarian to a technological society. Diversity is also increasing in the United States due to immigration (Manning, 2000). During the "Melting Pot" phase, everyone was expected to fit into a narrow definition of being American. However, as the United States moves toward a more pluralistic view, the definition of American also becomes broader. People from a variety of ethnic groups now maintain their ethnic and cultural identity as well as that of an American.

Therefore, as students from these different groups affirm their ethnic and cultural identities, it becomes imperative that educators include multicultural education in the curriculum. Multicultural education is not a course to be taken in school. It is about the lives of people from various groups, living in the United States. Multicultural education is about people. It is expected to deal with people with abilities and disabilities, people of different ages as well as people from different religions and social class. This is not to be confused with globalism which teaches about other cultures. Multicultural education is about various diverse groups in the United States and the contributions they have made to impact the culture. (Banks, 1990; Miller & Jacobson, 1994; Kobus, 1992; Baker, 1994; Ukpokodu,1999; Yeo, 1999).

Multicultural education, therefore, implies that instructional strategies should be representative of not only students in the classroom but also the communities represented in society. An environment that values multicultural education values diversity. In such an environment, therefore, there is a positive attitude toward differences. The curriculum in this type of environment is inclusive (Banks, 1990; Gollnick and Chinn, 2000; Manning, 2000).

Within the larger culture in the United States, however, there are several subcultures or microcultures that are included in the definition of multiculturalism. Although we all belong to the macroculture, people belong to a variety of microcultures. For example, people of different ages and races may belong to same religion or social class. Therefore, although there are numerous microcultures, for the purposes of education there are some that may be more impacting. These microcultures include age, ethnicity, exceptionality (ability/disability), gender, language, race, religion and social class. Effective multicultural curriculum, therefore, should help us think about, among other things, such things as ageism, gender bias, homophobia and ethnic, racial and religious prejudice and discrimination (Gollnick & Chinn, 2000).

Teacher Preparation and Multicultural Education

For the most part, many teachers have indicated a willingness to include multicultural education. However, as many teachers have indicated, they do not feel adequately prepared and, therefore, do not feel confident in including multicultural content in the curriculum Brown & Kysilka, 1994; Cannella & Reiff, 1994; Gallavan, 1998; Cruz-Janzen, 2000). Also, as Ukpokodu (1999) observed, many teachers were more inclined to teach from a global rather than a multicultural perspective. On investigation, the teachers' colleagues reported to Ukpokodu that many teachers felt uncomfortable dealing with multicultural issues because the issues are so sensitive. As a result, they were more inclined to teach globally.

The problems indicated by the teachers seem to begin with the preparation received. For example, in various studies of preservice teachers, the students have complained that their college of education programs do not adequately prepare them to work with diverse students or work in multicultural settings (Cannella & Reiff, 1994; Gallavan, 1998; Cooney & Akintunde, 1999). Preservice teachers have also indicated that many of the professors do not seem to have the background experience needed to authentically alert student to multicultural issues. The students also expressed that they felt the need for educators to have actually experienced diversity and discrimination in order to bring authenticity to their teaching (Cannella & Reiff, 1994; Gallavan, 1998; Cruz-Janzen, 2000).

However, Manning (2000), indicated that the problem goes beyond preparation. According to Manning (2000), the teacher's attitude toward diversity and students who are linguistically different is also a major part of the problem. According to Manning, teachers who approach diversity in the classroom with a negative attitude are likely to produce negative results. Manning suggests that students can detect the negative attitude teachers display. This attitude can interfere with the teacher's interaction with students as well as affect the teacher's ability to implement appropriate teaching-learning experiences. In the end, both the teacher and the students are impacted.

It is apparent, therefore, that college of education programs need to make a greater attempt to prepare teachers to be able to adequately integrate multicultural materials and activities into the curriculum. These programs also need to ensure that preservice teachers are helped to develop the ability to effectively work with diverse students as well as helped to effectively work in diverse settings.

Banks' Approaches to Content Integration

To assist teachers in the integration of ethnic content into the curriculum, Banks (1990), offered several approaches. According to Banks, the approaches commonly used by teachers are the Contributions Approach, the Heroes and Holidays Approach and the Ethnic Additive Approach. In these approaches the curriculum basically remains the same. There may be the addition of ethnic heroes or ethnic holidays, concepts, themes, a book or even a unit without any substantial change to the existing structure or goals of the curriculum. These are easy approaches and teachers who are not confident about content integration are more likely to use them.

However, Banks offers other approaches in which integration of content is likely to be much stronger. For example, the Transformation Approach infuses several ethnic perspectives. This, according to Banks, allows students to view issues, concepts and problems from various ethnic perspectives. This approach also allows students to gain a much better understanding of people and events and their impact on the culture of the United States, as it exists today. With this approach, students can begin to see the contributions of various ethnic groups and the ultimate changes that have taken place culturally.

Banks' last approach, the Decision-Making and Social Action Approach, encourages students to make a decision to take action based on a concept or problem that they have encountered. In this approach students develop critical thinking as they gather data, analyze problems and make a decision if any action should be taken. According to Banks, this empowers students as they begin to learn that they have the ability to take action and make changes based on their beliefs.

Banks does admit that one should not expect teachers to immediately move to the last approach. It takes time and practice. However, if teacher preparation programs begin to demonstrate how these approaches work, there is no question that student teachers will begin to see how they can transform the curriculum without sacrificing content, a fear which many teachers seem to have (Cannella & Reiff, 1994; Brown & Kysilka, 1994; Havas & Lucas, 1994; Gallavan, 1998). Also, these approaches will assist preservice and new teachers in creating educational objectives. The approaches will also ensure the integration of equitable material that will subsequently promote and empower all students regardless of their backgrounds (Cannella & Reiff, 1994; Aaronson, Carter & Howell, 1995; Gallavan, 1998; Cruz-Janzen, 2000).

What Are Some Benefits of Literature, Generally:

Although, generally, one of the best ways to gain information is direct involvement, children can learn about culture vicariously through books. There are also many other benefits to sharing books with children. Research has shown that children who are read to regularly and who are in an environment where reading is habitual and reinforced, tend to become early readers (Teale, 1984; Morrow, 2000).

Through interaction with books, children learn about language and they also learn how books function. Children also become familiar with print. The more exposure they get, the more they are able to distinguish between print and drawing as well as words and letters. They also learn about left to right progression which is the way books are read in English and some other languages. However, children can also be exposed to the up-down method used for Chinese and the right to left method used in Hebrew.

There is also the social aspect of reading to children. As the adult reads to the child there is social interaction and the adult is also able to scaffold for the child. Through adult support, the child is able to share and take turns reading words and pictures. The adult can expand on what the child says or extend by asking questions (Vygotsky's Zone of Proximal Development).

Research has also shown that the more exposure children have to books the more they are exposed to vocabulary words. This exposure helps with their own language development since words provide labels for things. They also learn that many labels may be appropriate for the same object (Goodman, 1986; Cazden, 1992; Morrow, 2000; Tomkins, 1998; Cox, 1999).

Reading can also help children develop thinking and comprehension skills. As they learn about the elements of story they may begin to question the plot and try to predict what comes next or what individual characters might have done differently.

As children listen to others read, they develop listening skills - auditory discrimination as well as visual discrimination which they will need for their own reading, if they are not yet readers. They learn to see the similarities and differences in letters and hear the similarities and differences in sounds. This enables them to begin to make associations.

Why Multicultural Children's Books?

In many ways multicultural children's books are no different from traditional mainstream books. The elements of story are usually the same and many of the concepts that children will learn are the same. However, there are also many differences. The background and experiences of characters are likely to be different and the way they dress is also likely to be different.

Children also tend to notice differences before they see similarities (Derman-Sparks, 2000; Seefeldt, 2001). It is, therefore, imperative to alert children to the fact we have similarities and, that where there are differences, it is not necessarily a negative thing. Multicultural children's books are an ideal way of exposing children to these similarities and differences.

Multicultural books add to children's experiences. They stimulate children's imagination. They will "visit" places they may never have been. For example, in the story *A River Ran Wild* (Cherry, 1992), children will be able to visualize the Nashua river and the problems that ensued as well as understand the importance of recycling. *The Crossroads* (Isadora, 1999), will assist children in learning about the lives of children in South Africa and the impact Apartheid had on their lives. Another books that can help children learn about a different culture is *Sam and the Lucky Money* (Chinn, 1995). This story alerts children to what is entailed in the traditional celebration of Chinese New Year. *A Carp for Kimiko* (Kroll, 1993), will assist children in learning about a Japanese celebration for boys called Children's Day. Ultimately, through these books, children learn how children in other cultures are like them, but also different.

Children also have the opportunity to learn about a subculture as evidenced in *The Talking Eggs* (San Souci, 1989). Also, in *Flossie and the Fox* (McKissack, 1986), for example, Flossie, in order to be able to evade the fox, asked her grandmother: "How do a fox look? Flossie asked. I disremember ever seeing one" (page 5). The content is sound. The reader is able to understand. However, for many readers, the language (dialect) may be unfamiliar because it is a southern dialect.

Children See Themselves Represented

Multicultural books also allow children to see themselves represented. Many children will have gone shopping with a grandparent and so they will be able to relate to *Not So Fast Songololo* (Daly, 1990). Some may have also gone with a grandparent who may be voting for the first time so they would be able to relate to *The Day My Gogo Went to Vote* (Sisulu, 1996). The voting circumstances are different since this author talks about Apartheid. However, there is the frame of reference that will, in the long run, assist children in understanding how a democracy works. Also, some children will be able to relate to difficulties some families are purported to have experienced during the United States Presidential election in 2000.

With regard to story context, when children see themselves represented in authentic ways, it helps to build their self esteem. They will also be able to relate to some difficulties experienced by other children and realize that other children experience the same things. For example, in the story *Did You Carry the Flag Today, Charlie?* (Caudhill, 1966), Charlie is having difficulty with the first days of school. He has difficulty meeting the contingency arrangement that would allow him to carry the flag. In *Cleversticks* (Ashley, 1991), a child feels inadequate because he cannot do what the other children can do. Soon, however, he realizes that he has a special skill. He can use chopsticks. In *Dumpling Soup* (Rattigan, 1993), a young Hawaiian girl is allowed to join in making dumplings for the soup as part of the New Year's Eve celebration. She is doing this for the first time and is worried that her dumplings will not come out right. Through this book the teacher will be able to assist the children in recognizing that we are all special in our own different ways, and we all experience anxiety at one time or another.

Illustrations

Illustrations are a very important part of literature for young children. Children who are not yet able to read conventionally will use the illustrations to assist them in reading the story. It is important, therefore, that the illustrations are well done so children can identify the characters (Jalongo 1992; Morrow, 2000).

It is important for children to see a true representation of themselves in books. For children who are not familiar with the characters, well done illustrations will assist them in learning about people who look different from the way they do. The illustrations should also be aesthetically pleasing so children will want to look at them. They should also be authentic. This is beneficial for both white and non white children. Teachers, therefore, should become acquainted with good illustrators. This will become useful when selecting books. When children, especially children from minority groups, see themselves in books they should be able to recognize and feel good about the people they see. Some badly illustrated books may create stereotypes. However, for good stories that are badly illustrated, teachers should discuss this with the children.

Types of Multicultural Children's Books

Children notice racial differences at a very early age. Their attitude towards difference is usually based on adult response. Children who see adults, especially significant adults, act comfortably towards differences are not likely to display discomfort. We, therefore, need to help children feel comfortable with differences and multicultural children's books provide one of the many ways to expose children to differences.

The types of multicultural books available are similar to mainstream trade books. Parents and teachers are, therefore, urged not to treat multicultural books as different or unique. Whether the books are concept books, participation books, traditional books, folktales and fairytales, biographies, predictable books, legends or wordless picture books, the story elements are likely to be the same. Human emotions are similar despite cultural, racial or other differences. The people and events represented may, however, be different and the reactions - the ways in which problems are resolved, are also likely be different. However, these are some of the things that define culture and children need to learn that.

It is important for children to realize that difference is not a deficit. Therefore, teachers should include as much diversity, as possible, in the classroom. Teachers can ensure that children are exposed to, and have an understanding of differences by making sure that they:

1.   Include a large variety of books in the classroom library. These books should represent diverse ethnic groups and cultures. Morrow (2000), suggests five to eight books per child. These books should include multicultural books.

2.   To assist children in becoming effective learners, it is important to have an environment that is nonthreatening. The environment should provide children, especially early and reluctant readers, with enough of a comfort level for taking risks. It is imperative, therefore, that teachers include a variety of multicultural books appropriate for a variety of reading and interest levels. This will allow children to feel comfortable exchanging difficult books for books they can manage, or even choosing easy books if those are the books in which they are interested.

3.   It is important that children know that there are several language symbol systems. Therefore, books in different languages, even those of children not represented in the classroom or the immediate community, should be included in the classroom..

Children will delight in being able to recognize and read these books or look at pictures. In the list of books provided in Appendix A, it should be noted that many of the authors have children's books in English as well as Spanish. Also to be noted is that some books that are available in English are also available in Spanish.

Multicultural books, materials and activities not only help to enlighten children but can also provide a catalyst, for preoperational children struggling with identity as well as mixed race and other children from various racial, ethnic and cultural groups for whom identity may be a problem.

Through multicultural literature, children will also begin to understand gender defined roles, the differences in families and differences in ability. In all of this they learn that differences are just that, differences. They also learn that although differences may define us at some level, they need not be the core of our being. Children also ultimately learn that, if they have a strong sense of who they are, they need not allow others to define them as was evidenced in the story *All Us Come Cross the Water* (Clifton, 1973).

Annotated Bibliography of
Multi-Cultural Children's Books

ADVENTURE/TRAVEL

Ambrus, Victor
THE THREE POOR TAILORS. Illus.
New York: Harcourt, Brace & World,
Inc., 1965. Three poor tailors decide to
visit the nearby town for the first time.
They get into trouble and try unsuc-
cessfully to escape on a nanny goat. Age:
5-8 years.

Bayles, C.A.
KEVIN CLOUD: CHIPPAWA BOY IN
THE CITY. Illus. Chicago: Reilly & Lee.
1972. The story of a Native American boy
in Chicago is told through the use of
photographs. Age: 6-8 years.

Caines, Jeannette
JUST US WOMEN. Illus: Pat Cummings.
New York: Gryphon House, 1990. Aunt
Martha, an African-American, bought a
new car and decided to drive to North
Carolina with her niece. The story
describes the trip taken by the two
women. Age: 4-8 years

Ets, Marie Hall
GILBERTO AND THE WIND. Illus.
New York: Viking Press, 1963. Gilberto,
a little Mexican boy, gives a description
of his activities with the wind which

appears as his playmate. He even knows
when the wind is tired so on such days he
lies beside the wind and rests. Age: 5-8

Freedman, Russell
BUFFALO HUNT. Illus. (With
photographs). New York: Holiday House,
1988. The role the buffalo played in the
lives of Native Americans is depicted.
The story also describes the preparation
that was necessary for the buffalo hunt.
Ages: 8-10 years.

Howard, Elizabeth Fitzgerald
THE TRAIN TO AUNT LULU'S. Illus:
Robert Casilla. New York: Aladdin
Books, 1994. Beppy and her younger
sister Babs, two African American girls,
are visiting their great aunt Lulu in
Baltimore. The children travel by train
and describe their nine-hour trip. Age: 6-9
years.

Kalman, Maira
SAYONARA, MRS. KACKLEMAN.
Illus: Maira Kalman. New York: Viking
Press, 1989. Alexander and his sister,
Lulu, finally visit Japan for their different
reasons. The story, as told by each of
them, describes their experiences while in
Japan. Age: 5-8 years.

1

Margolies, Barbara
REHEMA JOURNEY: A VISIT IN TANZANIA. Illus. Photographs. New York: Scholastic, Inc., 1990. Rehema Mfangavo gives the reader a tour of her country, Tanzania. Along with introducing family members and describing a trip into town, she describes life in Tanzania including foods that people eat. Age: 5-10 years

McVitty, Walter
ALI BABA AND THE FORTY THIEVES
Illus: Margaret Early. Abrams, 1989. A poor Arabian woodcutter discovers a cave with stolen wealth. He enters the cave by using the command, "Open Sesame!" Age: 5-10 years.

Rocard, Ann
KOUK AND THE ICE BEAR. Illus: Ann Morgan. Wilmington, DE.: Atomium Books, Inc., 1991. In this story, Kouk, a little Eskimo (Innuit) wants to play but all the adults are busy. He goes off and has a lot of fun. Then he meets the ice bear. Age: 6-10 years.

Rutland, Jonathan
TAKE A TRIP TO ISRAEL. Illus: Jonathan Rutland (photographs). London: Franklin Watts, 1981. Points out and briefly describes different prominent areas of Israel such as Galilee, River Jordan and Jerusalem. Age: 7-10 years.

Sandin, Joan
THE LONG WAY WESTWARD. Illus. Joan Sandin. New York: Harper, 1989. A Swedish family traveling from New York city to a small town in Minnesota encounter Svea Soc and some Swedish American families who help them. Age: 6-8 years.

Say, Allen
THE BICYCLE MAN. Illus. Allen Say. Boston: Houghton Mifflin Co., 1982. On sports day in a school yard in Japan, two American soldiers -one white and one black - appear. One soldier borrows the principal's bicycle and performs many tricks to the amazement and enjoyment of the teachers and children. Age:5-10 years.

Say, Allen
GRANDFATHER'S JOURNEY. Illus. Allen Say. New York: Scholastic Inc., 1993. The author describes his grandfather's journey. After returning to Japan to marry, the grandfather returns to the United States and settles in the San Francisco Bay before once again returning to Japan. Age: 6-9 years

Trease, Geoffrey
A FLIGHT OF ANGELS. Illus. New York: Lerner, 1989. Three friends find more than they bargain for when they decide to explore the limestone caves under the city of contemporary Nottingham for their research. Age: 8-10 years.

Yashima, Taro
THE VILLAGE TREE. Illus. New York: Viking Press, 1953. A huge tree, which stands over the river in a village in Japan, provides shade as well as interesting activities for the children. Age: 7 years and older.

ALPHABET

Bond, J. C.
A IS FOR AFRICA. Illus. New York: Watts, 1989. Using photographs of the people and artifacts, the book introduces the reader to the alphabet and various aspects of life in different countries of Africa. Age: 5-8 years

Feelings, Muriel
JAMBO MEANS HELLO. Illus: Tom Feelings. New York: Dial press, 1974. African life and customs are described through the alphabet. The English equivalent is given for the Swahili version. Age: 5-8 years.

Feeney, Stephanie
A IS FOR ALOHA. Illus: Photographs by Hella Hammid. The University Press of Hawaii (A Kolowalu Book), 1980. An ABC book about Hawaii. Each letter of the alphabet represents something in Hawaii. Age: 4-8 years.

Fife, Dale
ADAM'S ABC. Illus: Don Robertson.. New York: Coward McCann & Geoghegan, Inc., 1971. Adam, an African American boy, lives in the city in the same apartment building as his two friends. The alphabet is used to take us through activities in which they become involved. Age: 6-8 years.

Owoo, Ife Nii
A IS FOR AFRICA. Illus. Ife Nii Owoo. Africa World Press Inc., 1992. Using pictures the author exposes the reader to various aspects of life and culture in Africa through the alphabet. Age: 3-6 years.

Rosario, I.
INDALIA'S PROJECT ABC. Illus. New York: Holt, Rinehart & Winston, 1987. In this story there is a mixture of African-American and Hispanic life. The scenes are definitely urban with the alphabet in English and Spanish. Age: 6 and older.

ANIMALS

Anderson, John Lonso
IZZARD. Illus: Adrienne Adams. New York: Charles Scribner's Sons, 1973. Jamie, a little Black boy who lives in the Virgin Islands, becomes attached to the lizard that had hatched in his hand. Later, however, the lizard finds other lizards and spends more time with them much to Jamie's disappointment. Age: 7-8 years.

Appleby, Ellen
THE THREE BILLY GOATS GRUFF. Illus. New York: Gryphon House, 1990. A Norwegian tale about three billy goats trying to outsmart a mean troll to get to the other side of the bridge where the grass is greener. Age: 4-8 years.

Carle, Eric
THE VERY HUNGRY CATERPILLAR. New York: Philomel Books, 1969. The reader follows the caterpillar as he eats from Monday to Sunday before having its metamorphosis into a butterfly. The type of food changes and the number increases each day of the week. Age: 4-8.

Eastman, Philip
ARE YOU MY MOTHER. Illus: P.D. Eastman. New York: Random House, Inc., 1960. A mother bird leaves her nearly hatched egg to find food for the

new arrival. The baby bird is hatched and leaves the nest to find mother only he does not know what mother looks like. Age: 5-7 years.

Geraghty, Paul
OVER THE STEAMY SWAMP. Illus. New York: Gryphon House, 1990. As the animals in a swamp in Africa get hungry they go from prey to predator. The "food chain" starts with the mosquito then moves to the other animals. Age: 3-7 years.

Goennel, Heidi
IF I WERE A PENGUIN. Illus. New York: Gryphon House, 1990. Children are given the opportunity to imagine themselves as animals from different parts of the world -- animals from cold as well as warm regions.
Age: 3-6 years.

Hart, Trish
THERE ARE NO POLAR BEARS DOWN THERE. Illus: Trish Hart. New York: Macmillan McGraw-Hill School Publishing Co., 1994. A short twelve-page, easy-to-read book which tells what type of animals live in Antarctica - but there are no polar bears. Age: 3-6 years.

Keats, Ezra Jack
HI, CAT! Illus. New York: The Macmillan Co., 1970. This story takes place in a Hispanic neighborhood. A cat decides to stick with Archie who made the mistake of saying 'hi!' to the cat. The cat becomes a nuisance and scares away the audience at a performance put on by Archie and his friend Peter.
Age: 3-8 years.

Kipling, Rudyard
HOW THE RHINOCEROS GOT HIS SKIN. Illus. Tim Raglin. Rabbit Ears Books, MA. 1988. The Parsee man bakes his cake and as he is about to eat it an ill-mannered rhinoceros comes by and eats it. The Parsee man vows revenge which he takes in an unusual way. Age 3-8 years.

Mayer, Mercer
WHAT DO YOU DO WITH A KANGAROO? Illus: Mercer Mayer. New York: Four Winds Press, 1973. A little girl is continually disturbed by animals from different cultural groups such as a kangaroo, a camel and a llama who make demands on her. She tells what should be done with each of them. Finally when they take her bed she goes to sleep beside them. Age: 5-8 years.

Otsuka, Yuzo (Adapted from the translation by Ann Herring).
SUHO AND THE WHITE HORSE Illus: Suekichi Akaba. New York: The Viking Press, 1981. A Mongolian story about a little boy who finds a white colt and raises it but the colt is taken from him by the Mayor. The colt eventually dies so the boy then does something special to preserve the memory of the colt. Age: 7-10 years.

Polacco, Patricia
JUST PLAIN FANCY. Illus: Patricia Polacco. New York: Dell Publishing, 1990.Naomi, a young Amish girl, has the responsibility of taking care of the chickens. She keeps wishing for something fancy. One day she finds an unusual egg and things take a totally different turn. Age 3-10 years.

Sis, Peter
KOMODO. Illus: Peter Sis. New York: Greenwillow Books, 1993. A little boy and his parents travel to Indonesia in search of seeing a Komodo dragon. Age: 6-10 years.

Thompson, Vivian L.
KEOLA'S HAWAIIAN DONKEY. Illus: Earl Thollander. San Carlos, California: Golden Gate Junior Books, 1966. The donkey is named Pakiki because his master considers him stubborn. Keola discovers, however, that the donkey is not stubborn but like him enjoys watching the beautiful sights of Hawaii. He then changes the donkey's name to Akamai, the Wise One. Age: 8 years and older.

Tsuchiya, Yukio
FAITHFUL ELEPHANTS: A TRUE STORY OF ANIMALS, PEOPLE AND WAR. Illus: Ted Lewin. New York: Houghton, 1988. During World War 11, Japanese zoo keepers are forced to kill the elephants for fear that they may escape and trample people during a bombing. Age: 7-9 years.

Uchida, Yoshiko
THE TWO FOOLISH CATS. Illus: Margot Zemach. New York: Margaret K. Mc Elderry Books, 1987. This is a Japanese tale about the fight between two hungry cats after they find they cannot not agree as to who should get the larger rice cakes. They go to monkey for advice and are tricked out of their food.
Age: 6-10 years.

BIOGRAPHY

Adler, David
A PICTURE BOOK OF SOJOURNER TRUTH. Illus: Gershom Griffith.. New York: Holiday House, 1994. The early life of Sojourner Truth as well as her life as a slave and abolitionist is described. Age: 7-10 years.

Brooks, Philip
MICHAEL JORDAN: BEYOND AIR. Illus: Philip Brooks. Illinois: Chicago Press, 1995. Describes the struggles of Michael Jordan and the struggles he faced as a black baseball player. Age: 6-10 years.

Coerr, Eleanor
SADAKO. Illus: Ed Young. New York: Putnam & Grosset Group, 1997. Sadako Sasaki died at the age of twelve years from leukemia - a result of the bombing of Hiroshima in 1945. She tried to fold one thousand cranes in the belief that that would make her better. Age: 7 and older.

Cooper, Floyd
COMING HOME. Illus: Floyd Cooper. New York: Philomel Books, 1994. Langston Hughes, internationally known writer/poet had a difficult childhood. His life is described in this story. Age: 7-10 years.

Cooper, Floyd
MANDELA. Illus: Floyd Cooper. New York: Philomel Books, 1996. The story is of the life of Mandela from boyhood to his ultimate release from prison. Readers

will learn a little about the life of blacks in South Africa during Apartheid and Mandela's fight for fair treatment. Age: 6 and older.

Hoyt-Goldsmith, Diane
HOANG ANH: A VIETNAMESE-AMERICAN BOY. Photographs by Lawrence Migdale. New York: Holiday House, 1992. Hoang Anh is a Vietnamese American boy. He was born in a refugee camp in Malaysia prior to arrival in the United States. Hoang Anh describes his family's new life and shares similarities and traditions of Vietnam. Age: 7 and older.

Kilborne, Sarah
LEAVING VIETNAM: THE TRUE STORY OF TUAN NGO. Illus: Melissa Sweet. New York: Simon and Schuster, 1999. Tuan and his father flee Vietnam for the United States during the war. Eventually they are able to send for the rest of the family. Age: 8-10.

Kupperstein, Joel
CELEBRATING MARTIN LUTHER KING, JR. DAY. Illus: Fred Willingham. New York: Creative Teaching Press, Inc., 1999. Describes in very simple language the life of Martin Luther King, Jr. Age: 5-8.

Lepscky, Ibi
LEONARDO DA VINCI. Illus: Paolo Cardoni. New York: Barrons, 1984. Describes the life of Leonardo da Vinci, the Italian painter. Age: 6-10 years.

Marzollo, Jean
HAPPY BIRTHDAY MARTIN LUTHER KING, JR. Illus: J. Brown Pinkney. New York: Scholastic, Inc., 1993. This story describes the life of Martin Luther King growing up and the struggles he faced. Age: 6-8 years.

McKissack, Patricia
JESSE JACKSON: A BIOGRAPHY. Illus. photographs. New York: Scholastic Inc., 1989. Chronicles the life of Jesse Jackson, an African-American including some of the controversies. Age: 8 years and older.

Miller, William
ZORA HURSTON AND THE CHINABERRY TREE. Illus: Cornelius Van Wright and Ying-Hwa Hu. New York: Lee and Low Books, Inc., 1994. Zora's mother taught her to climb the chinaberry tree in order to see far away places. Before her mother's death, Zora promises her mother that she will one day visit and write about these places. Age 6-10 years

O'Connor, Jim
JACKIE ROBINSON AND THE STORY OF ALL-BLACK BASEBALL. Illus. Jim Butcher. New York: Random House, 1989. This story discusses the life of Jackie Robinson, an African-American. The problems he faced as an African American baseball player are also described. Age: 7-9 years.

Polacco, Patricia
PINK AND SAY. Illus: Patricia Polacco. New York: Philomel Books, 1994. Pinkus Aylee, a young Black soldier got separated from his unit. As he made the long trek home he met Say, a young White soldier who had deserted his unit. A friendship is formed until they were captured by the Confederate army. Age: 6 year and older.

Rappaport, Doreen
MARTIN'S BIG WORDS. Illus: Bryan Collier. New York: Jump At The Sun Press, 2001. Martin Luther King, Jr. is awed by his father's preaching and hopes to be like his father one day. Age: 5-9 years.

Rowley, John
HARRIET TUBMAN. Illus: John Rowley. New York: Heineman Interactive Library, 1998. Describes the life of Harriet Tubman and her attempts to help slaves through the Underground Railroad. Age: 6-8 years.

'Schroeder, Alan
RAGTIME TUMPIE. Illus: Bernie Fuchs. Joy Street/Little, 1989. Describes the life of Josephine Baker, an African American singer, who could not make it in the United States. She, therefore, goes to Paris where she becomes a famous Jazz singer and dancer. Age: 4-6 years.

Tatsuharu, Kodama
SHIN'S TRICYCLE. Illus: Noriyuki Ando. New York: Walker & Co., 1995. Shin Tetsutani always wanted a tricycle. Shin's uncle finally gave him the tricycle for his birthday. Hiroshima was bombed two weeks before his fourth birthday and he was killed. Age: 6 and older.

Thompson, Marguerite C.
DR. MARTIN LUTHER KING, JR: A STORY FOR CHILDREN. Illus: Alex Castro. New York: Gryphon House, 1990. A short story of the life of Dr. Martin Luther King, Jr., an African-American who was a prominent figure in the Civil Rights Movement. Age: 4-8 years.

West, Alan
ROBERTO CLEMENTE: BASEBALL LEGEND. Illus: (Various). New York: The Millbrook Press, 1993. Describes the life of Roberto Clemente, the first nationally known Latino (Puerto Rican) baseball player. Age: 7-10.

Wright, David
VIETNAM IS MY HOME. Illus: Kristi Ludwig. New York: Gareth Stevens Publishing, 1993. Ho Thi Kim Chau is an eleven year-old Vietnamese girl. The story describes her life in the little village where she lives outside Ho Chi Minh city. Age 7-10

CLOTHING

Beskow, Elsa
PELLE'S NEW SUIT. Illus: Elsa Beskow. New York: Harper Row Publishers, 1979. Pelle, a little Swedish boy, realizing that he was growing out of his clothes, decides to do something about it. Pelle shears the sheep and then trades his labor with different people in order to get the wool carded to make a new suit. Age: 7-9 years

de Paola, Tomie
CHARLIE NEEDS A CLOAK. Illus: Tomie de Paola. Englewood Cliffs, New Jersey: Prentice Hall, Inc., 1973. Charlie, a shepherd, needs a new cloak. The story describes how Charlie shears his sheep, washes, cards and spins the wool into yarn to make his cloak. Age: 3-6 years.

Gilman, Phoebe
SOMETHING FROM NOTHING. Illus: Phoebe Gilman. New York: Scholastic, Inc., 1992. Joseph's grandfather made him a blanket when he was a baby. As Joseph gets older, the blanket gets tattered and is made into different items. Ages 5-8.

Keats, Ezra Jack
JENNIE'S HAT. Illus: Ezra Jack Keats. New York: Harper Trophy, 1966. Jennie goes to the park on Sundays to feed the birds. They expect her. When Jennie got a new hat she did not like the birds help her to decorate it. Age: 3-6 years.

Munsch, Robert
THOMAS'S SNOWSUIT. Illus: Michael Martchenko. Annick Press, 1985. This story is about Thomas, a little boy in Canada, who doesn't want to put on his snowsuit. The teacher, and then the principal, intervene and each ends up wearing the snowsuit.
Age: 3-8 years.

Parton, Dolly
COAT OF MANY COLORS. Illus: Judith Sutton. New York: Scholastic, Inc., 1994. Dolly's mother made her a coat from scraps of cloth but when she proudly wore the coat to school the children laughed at her because the coat signified her poverty. Age: 5-8.

Ziefert, Harriet
A NEW COAT FOR ANNA. Illus: Anita Lobel. New York: Alfred A Knopf, Anna needs a new coat. The war is over but Anna's mother has no money so a series of trades are made so Anna can have a coat for winter. Age: 3-8 years.

COMMUNITY PRIDE

Cherry, Lynne
A RIVER RAN WILD: AN ENVIRONMENTAL HISTORY. Illus: Lynne Cherry. New York: Harcourt Brace Jovanovich, Publishers, 1992. The Nashua finally find a place to settle. They call it the Nash-A-Way. However, during the Industrial Revolution the river is polluted and it stays that way until the native people are able to convince community members to help to clean up this once beautiful river.
Age: 8 and older.

Fleishman, Paul
SEEDFOLKS. Illus: Judy Pedersen. New York: Joanna Coulter Books/Harper Trophy, 1997. An empty trash-filled lot in an urban area is soon transplanted when a Korean girl has the idea to plant lima beans. Age 9 and older.

Guthrie, Donna
A ROSE FOR ABBY. Illus. Dennis Hockerman. New York: Gryphon House, 1990. Abbie, an African-American tries to get members of her community to help the homeless. Age: 4-8 years.

COOPERATION

Oppenheim, Jeanne
ON THE OTHER SIDE OF THE RIVER.
Illus: Aliki. London: Franklin Watts Inc.,
1972. The European village of Wynlock-
On-The-River is joined only by a bridge.
The people on the different sides did not
get along. When the bridge collapses they
realize how much they need each other.
Age: 5-8 years.

COUNTING

Feelings, Muriel
MOJA MEANS ONE: SWAHILI
COUNTING BOOK. Illus: Tom Feelings.
New York: The Dial Press, 1971. Along
with the number and the Swahili word for
that number, each page gives a
description of life in Africa. Age: 6- 8
years.

Winter, Jeanette
JOSEFINA. Illus: Jeanette Winter. New
York: Harcourt Brace and Co., 1996.
Josefina, a Mexican sculptor, works in her
patio making artifacts out of clay. She
starts with one sun and finally ten stars.
The items are then displayed sequentially,
from one to ten, on her patio. Age 4-10
years.

FAMILY

Adoff, Arnold
BLACK IS BROWN IS TAN. Illus:
Pictures by Emily Arnold McCully. New
York: Harper Trophy, 1973. This is the
story of an interracial family. The story is
told in humorous, poetic form and lots of
comparisons are made to the color of
family members and everyday items. Age
4-8 years.

Armstrong, William H.
SOUNDER. New York: Harper, Row
Publishers, 1989. This is the story of a
black sharecropping family struggling to
survive in the South. It is also about
Sounder, the family's devoted dog, and
the tragedy that beset them when the
father is caught stealing food for the
family. Age: 9 and older.

Barker, Carol
A FAMILY IN NIGERIA. Photographs
by Carol Barker. New York: Lerner
Publications Co. 1985. Through Thaddeus
we taken into the day-to-day life of a
Nigerian (Yoruba) family. Age: 7-10
years.

Bunting, Eve
GOING HOME. Illus: David Diaz. New
York: Harper Collins Publishers, 1996. A
Mexican migrant family return to Mexico
to show their children a part of their
heritage.
Age: 6-10 Years.

Bunting, Eve
JIN WOO. Illus: Chris Soentpiet. New
York: Clarion Books, 2001. David is
jealous of his baby brother, Jin Woo, who
is Korean. He gets a letter from Jin Woo
assuring him that their parents love them
equally.
Age: 3-8 years.

Carter, Dorothy
WILHE'MINA MILES AFTER THE
STORK NIGHT. Illus: Harvey Stevenson.
New York: Frances Foster Books, 1999.

Wilhe'mina's father is out of town and her mother is about to deliver a baby so Wilhe'mina has to go get help in the dark of night. Age: 6 and older.

Clifton, Lucille
AMIFIKA. Illus: Thomas DiGrazia. New York: E.P. Dutton, 1977. Amifika, a little African-American boy overhears a conversation between his mother and his cousin regarding the return of his father from the army. He misunderstands and runs away but is soon found. He is reunited with his father whom he then remembers. Age: 6-8 years.

Clifton, Lucille
EVERETT ANDERSON'S NINE MONTH LONG. Illus: Ann Grifalconi. New York: Henry Holt and Co., 1978. Everett Anderson's mother has remarried and is about to have a baby. Everett is feeling left out but is reassured of his mother's love by his stepfather. Age: 5-8 years.

Cosby, Bill
THE DAY I SAW MY FATHER CRY. Illus: Varnette P. Honeywood. New York: Scholastic, Inc., 2000. Lil' Bill and his brother are always fighting. However, when a close friend of the family dies they understand how trivial their problems are and make a change.
Age: 5-10 years.

Cowen-Fletcher, Jane
IT TAKES A VILLAGE. Illus. Jane Cowen-Fletcher. New York: Scholastic Inc., 1994. Yemi has the responsibility to take care of her brother, Kokou, as her mother sells in the market. Kokou disappears and Yemi learns that it takes more than one person to take care of a child. Age 4-8 years.

Heide, Florence Parry
TIO ARMANDO. Illus: Ann Grifalconi. New York: Lothrop, Lee and Shepard Books, 1998. Uncle Armando, who is Mexican, teaches his nieces and nephews about the Mexican way of celebrating the death of loved ones. Age: 6-10 years.

Hoffman, Mary
BOUNDLESS GRACE: THE SEQUEL TO AMAZING GRACE. Illus. Caroline Binch. New York: Scholastic Inc.,1995. Grace feels her family is not complete because she has no father. When her father sends her a ticket for two to Gambia she goes with her grandmother and discovers family is what you make it. Ages 5-8 years.

Howard, Elizabeth Fitzgerald
AUNT FLOSSIE'S HATS AND CRAB CAKES LATER. Illus. James Ransome. New York: Scholastic Inc., 1991. Sarah and Susan, two African-American girls love to visit Aunt Flossie and hear stories about her hats. Along with the stories is the trip for crab cakes which the girls also enjoyed. Age 5-8 years.

Isadora, Rachel
AT THE CROSSROADS. Illus. Rachel Isadora. New York: Scholastic Inc., 1991. After their fathers have been away for ten months working in the mines, some South African children wait all night at the crossroads for their return. Age 8 and older.

Jacobson, Peter Otto & Kristensen, Preben
A FAMILY IN THAILAND. Illus. (photographs) The Bookwright Press, 1986. Using one family, life in Thailand is described including the food - especially the various types of fruits available. Age: 8-10 years.

Jenness, Aylette
IN TWO WORLDS: A YUP'IK ESKIMO FAMILY. Illus.(photographs). Aylette Jenness. New York: Houghton Mifflin, 1989. After twenty years the author returns to a coastal village. The changes and how they have affected the residents are described through the lives of the Rivens family.
Age: 8 and older.

Joose, Barbara M.
MAMA, DO YOU LOVE ME? Illus: Barbara Lavallee. San Francisco: Chronicle Books, 1991. An Innuit child tests her mother to find out under what conditions her mother would stop loving her. She learns that her mother's love is unconditional. Age: 3 -8 years.

Keats, Ezra Jack
LOUIE'S SEARCH. Illus: Ezra Jack Keats. New York: Macmillan Publishing, 1980. Louie sets out to search for a father. However, a music box which falls off a truck and is retrieved by Louie, changes Louie's life. Age: 5-8 years.

Keats, Ezra Jack
PETER'S CHAIR. Illus: Ezra jack Keats New York: Harper & Row Publishers, 1967. In this Hispanic family, the arrival of Peter's baby sister, Susie, brings jealousy over a chair. Peter soon discovers that he is now too big for the chair which helps to reconcile him. Age: 3-8 years.

Levinson, Riki
OUR HOME IS THE SEA. Illus.(photographs). New York: Gryphon House, 1990. Living in a house boat is a part of the ancient Japanese culture. In this story a little boy's life is portrayed as ancient and modern as he moves back and forth from the streets of Hong Kong to the houseboat.
Age: 3-7 years.

McDonald, Joyce
THE MAIL-ORDER KID. Illus: Joyce McDonald. Putnam, 1988. Flip, a fifth grader, is irritated by the six year old Korean boy his mother has adopted. Later, when he orders a fox by mail, he sees the adjustment that has to be made . Age: 8-10.

Mitchell, Margaree King
UNCLE JED'S BARBERSHOP. Illus: James Ransome. New York: Scholastic Inc., 1993. Uncle Jed had a dream of opening a barbershop. After many setbacks, he opens his own barbershop on his seventy ninth birthday much to his delight and that of his customers. Age: 5 years and older.

Pellegrini, Nina
FAMILIES ARE DIFFERENT. Illus: Nina Pellegrini. New York: Scholastic, Inc., 1991. A little Koren girl is adopted into an American family. She is unhappy because she feels different. However, she soon learns that all families are different. Age: 6-10 years.

Pinkney, Gloria Jean
BACK HOME. Illus: Jerry Pinkney. New York: Dial Books for Young Readers, 1992. Ernestine, an African-American girl, returns to the North Carolina farm where she was born. She learns much about farm life, even from her cousin who is sometimes quite disgusted with her lack of rural knowledge. Age: 6 and older.

Rowland, Florence Wightman
AMISH WEDDING. Illus: Dale Parsons. New York: G. P. Putnam's Sons, 1971. Jonathan, an Amish boy, describes the courtship and wedding of his sister Rebecca. Age: 7-10 years.

Rosenberg, Maxine
LIVING IN TWO WORLDS. Illus: Georgie Ancona (photographs). New York: Lothrop, Lee & Shepard Books, 1986. A book about bi-racial families. The children share the advantages and disadvantages of belonging to two cultures. Age: 8 years and older.

Rylant, Cynthia
THE RELATIVES CAME. Illus: Stephen Gammell. New York: Gryphon House, 1990. Poor White family members from the Rural South, decide to visit relatives in the North. The book describes the difference in the lifestyle of the relatives. Age: 3-7 years.

Say, Allen
TEA WITH MILK. Illus: Allen Say. New York: Houghton Mifflin Co., 1999. A Japanese American girl is taken back to Japan by her parents but she prefers the American way. Soon she meets someone who is more like her and who also speaks English. Age: 7-10 years.

Shannon, Terry
CHILDREN IN A CHANGING WORLD: CHILDREN OF HONG KONG. Illus. Charles Payzant (photographs). Chicago: Children's Press, 1975. The life and customs of the people in Hong Kong are described through children. Some of the boat people have to come ashore to attend school and the children of foreigners have to adjust to the differences. Age: 7-8 years

Sobol, Harriet Langsam
WE DON'T LOOK LIKE OUR MOM AND DAD. Illus: Patricia Agre (photographs). New York: Coward-McCann, Inc., 1984. Eric and John are two Korean boys adopted by an American family, the Levins. Issues related to adoption are discussed by the family. Age: 6-10 years

Sonneborn, Ruth
FRIDAY NIGHT IS PAPA NIGHT Illus: Emily A. McCully. New York: Gryphon House, 1990. An Hispanic boy, Pedro, is excited. His father is able to come home only on Friday nights. It is now Friday and this means Pedro will get to be with his father. Age: 3-7 years.

Soto, Gary
SNAPSHOTS FROM THE WEDDING. Illus: Stephanie Garcia. New York: G. P. Putnam & Sons, 1997. Maya, a little Hispanic girl is a flower girl in a wedding. In this story she describes her family members and the wedding. Age: 5-8 years.

Stanek, Muriel
I SPEAK ENGLISH FOR MY MOM. Illus: Judith Friedman. Chicago, Ill.: Albert Whitman Co., 1989. Lupe is a

Mexican American girl who speaks Spanish at home, English at school and she speaks English for her mother when they are out together. When the mother's job gets insecure she decides to learn English. Age: 5-10 years.

Thomas, Jane Resh
LIGHTS ON THE RIVER. Illus: Michael Dooling. New York: Hyperion Paperbacks for Children, 1996. Theresa's parents, aunt and uncle are Mexican-American migrant workers. As they travel around to find work they experience many hardships. To brighten her experience, Theresa recalls memories in Mexico with her Abuela. Age: 6 and older.

Williams, Vera B.
A CHAIR FOR MY MOTHER. Illus: Vera B. Williams. New York: Scholastic Inc., 1982. After losing their furniture in a fire, neighbors help to replace all needed items except a well needed comfy chair. A little girl saves her pennies to help her mother buy such a chair. Age: 6-8 years.

FEAR/COURAGE

Asch, Frank
HERE COMES THE CAT. Illus: Vladimir Vagin. New York: Gryphon House, 1990. This is a Russian story (in English), about a mouse who is afraid of the cat. The mouse takes the job of warning his friends when the cat is coming only to learn that there really is nothing to fear. Age: 3-7years.

Berry, James
A THIEF IN THE VILLAGE AND OTHER STORIES. Illus. Orchard Watts,

1988. In these nine short stories, some Jamaican children encounter many hardships. For example, two children try to protect their orchard against thieves. Age: 8 and older.

Bishop, Claire & Wiese, Kurt
THE FIVE CHINESE BROTHERS
Illus. New York: Coward-McCann, Inc., 1968. One of five Chinese brothers with special skills gets himself in trouble with the law. The story tells how the four brothers help to save him. Age: 6-8 years

Bornstein, Ruth Lercher
OF COURSE A GOAT. Illus: Ruth Lercher Bornstein. New York: Harper & Row Publishers, 980. In this European story, a little boy wants a goat. He is encouraged by his mother to go on the mountain to get it. The little boy is afraid but is assured by his mother that she will be there when he returns. Age: 7-9 years.

DeArmond, Dale
THE SEAL OIL LAMP. Illus. Dale DeArmond. Sierra Club/Little, 1988. Allugua, who is blind, is left to die according to the laws of his native Alaskan people. However, he shows kindness to a freezing mouse and his life changes. Age: 6-10 years

Fenner, Carol
ICE SKATES. Illus. Ati Forberg. New York: Scholastic Inc., 1978. Marsha, an African-American girl, dreams of skating except the skater in her dreams look nothing like her. She is given skates for Christmas and finally learns to skate. Age: 5-8 years.

Grifalconi, Ann
DARKNESS AND THE BUTTERFLY.
Illus. New York: Gryphon House, 1990.
Osa is a young African girl who is afraid
of the dark. With the help of a beautiful
yellow butterfly and a wise old woman
she learns to overcome her fear. Age: 4-8
years.

Keats, Ezra Jack
DREAMS. Illus: Ezra Jack Keats. New
York: MacMillan Publishing Co., 1974.
Roberto, a little Hispanic boy, made a
paper mouse which he left on his window
sill after showing it to Amy, his neighbor.
Later that night the mouse helps to stop a
fight, between a dog and a cat, in the
street of this Hispanic neighborhood .
Age: 5-8 Years.

Keats, Ezra Jack
GOGGLES. Illus: Ezra Jack Keats. New
York: Macmillan Publishing Co., 1969.
Archie and His friend Peter, two Hispanic
boys, find a pair of motorcycle goggles.
Some bullies try to take it but are
outwitted. Age: 3-8 years.

Moskin, Marietta D.
TOTO. Illus: Rocco Negri. New York:
Coward, McCann & Geoghegan, Inc.,
1971. Toto, an elephant and Suku, a
young African boy, are both protected by
adults. Through the same event they
wander beyond their existing boundaries
and gain courage by the experience. Age:
7-9 years.

Seger, Pete
ABIYOYO: BASED ON A SOUTH
AFRICAN LULLABY AND FOLK
STORY. Illus: Michael Hays. New York:
Macmillan Publishing Co.1986. A young
boy with a ukelele and his magician father
are banished to the edge of town.
However, when they manage to get rid of
Abiyoyo, the feared giant, they are
heartily welcomed back into town. Age: 3
and older.

Stanley, Diane & Vennema, P.
SHAKA: KING OF THE ZULUS. Illus.
Diane Stanley. New York: Morrow, 1988.
Shaka, an outcast, rises to eventually
become Chief of an African tribe. Age: 7-
9 years.

Stolz, Mary
STORM IN THE NIGHT. Illus: Pat
Cummings. Harper & Row, 1988. The
lights go out during a storm. Thomas, a
young African American boy, pretends
not to be afraid. His grandfather, however,
tells of a similar incident in his life which
helps Thomas to understand fear and
human nature. Age: 5-8 years.

Winter, Jeanette
FOLLOW THE DRINKING GOURD.
Illus.
New York: Alfred A. Knopf, 1988. This
story tells how Peg Leg Joe, a conductor
for the Underground Railroad, helps a
group of black slaves escape to freedom
by following the Big Dipper. Age: 6 and
older.

Yolen, Jane
THE EMPEROR AND THE KITE. Illus.
Ed Young (pictures). New York: William
Collins & World Publishing Co., 1982.
Djeow Seow, the youngest and the most
ignored child in the Emperor's Chinese
family, saves her captured father through
the helpful words of a monk and the use
of a kite. Age: 6-8 years.

FEELINGS/EMOTIONS

Barrett, Joyce Durham
WILLIE'S NOT THE HUGGING KIND.
Illus. Pat Cummings. New York: Harper
Trophy, 1989. Willie, an African-
American boy, wants to be like his friend
Jo Jo so he decides hugging is silly. But
Willie longs for a hug so he finally gives
in to his need.
Age: 5-8 years.

Johnson, Tony
THE QUILT STORY. Illus. Tomie De
Paola. New York: Scholastic Inc., 1985.
A little girl's mother makes her a quilt.
Later, another girl becomes owner of the
quilt and she becomes as attached to the
quilt as the previous owner. Age: 5-8
years.

FOLKTALE/FAIRYTALE/FABLE

Aardema, Verna
ANANSI FINDS A FOOL. Illus. Bryna
Waldman. New York: Dial Books for
Young Readers, 1992. In this Ashanti
folktale, Anansi wants someone to go
fishing with him. He wants his partner to
do the work while he gets the fish.
However, Anansi is outwitted by his
friend Bonsu. Age: 5-8 years.

Aardema, Verna
BIMWILI AND THE ZIMWI: A TALE
FROM ZANZIBAR. Illus: Susan
Maddaugh. New York: Dial Books, 1985.
A little Swahili girl goes with her sisters
to play by the sea and is captured by the
Zimwi. Age: 4-8 years.

Aardema, Verna (Retold by)
BORREGUITA AND THE COYOTE: A
TALE FROM AYUTLA, MEXICO. Illus:
Petra Mathers. New York: Scholastic,
Inc., 1991. A Mexican folktale of
Borreguita, a little lamb, that constantly
outwits a coyote who is determined to eat
her. Age: 5 and older.

Aardema, Verna
OH, KOJO! HOW COULD YOU! (An
Ashanti Tale). Illus: Marc Brown. New
York: Dial Books for Yong Readers,1984.
Kojo is constantly fooled into buying
useless animals from the trickster Ananse.
However, when Ananse sells Kojo a
seemingly useless dove, it is Ananse who
becomes the loser. Age: 4 years and older.

Aardema, Verna
RABBIT MAKES A MONKEY OF
LION: A SWAHILI TALE. Illus: Jerry
Pinkney. New York: Dial Press, 1989. In
this East African tale, rabbit, once again,
outwits lion who is trying to catch him for
robbing his honey store a second time.
Ages 5-7 years.

Aardema, Verna
WHY MOSQUITOES BUZZ IN
PEOPLE'S EARS. Illus: Leo & Diane
Dillon (pictures). New York: The Dial
Press, 1975. A West African folktale
about a mosquito who after telling a tall
tale, causes a series of problems for the
other animals. Eventually, the mosquito is
forgiven but now instead of telling tall
tales he buzzes in people's ears asking
forgiveness. Age: 7-8 years.

Alexander, Ellen
LLAMA AND THE GREAT FLOOD.
Illus: Ellen Alexander. New York:
Gryphon House, 1990. This Andean story
explains how llama saves both people
and animals during the great flood. Age 4-
8 years.

Anderson, Hans Christian
SWINEHERD: A DANISH FOLKTALE
(Translated from Danish by Althea Bell).
Illus: Lisbeth Zwerger. Picture Book
Studio USA., 1985. A prince wants to
marry the Emperor's daughter but he soon
finds out what the princess is like and
changes his mind. Age: 6-10 years.

Berry, James
SPIDERMAN ANANCY. Illus: Joseph
Olubo. New York: Henry Holt &
Company. 1988. This is the retelling of
twenty Caribbean and West African
folktales in which Anancy, the
Spiderman, is up to his usual tricks in an
attempt to outwit everyone. Age: 8-10
years.

Brett, Jan
THE MITTEN. Illus: Jan Brett. New
York: Putnam Publishing Co., 1989. This
Ukranian folktale is about a little boy who
after insisting on getting white mittens is
knitted a pair by his grandmother. The
story is about one of the mittens which the
boy loses. Age: 4-7 years.

Brown, Marcia
STONE SOUP. Illus: Marcia Brown. New
York: Aladdin Books, 1986. Three French
soldiers outwit some villagers who are
unwilling to provide them with food and
lodging. Age: 5 and older.

Broughton, Joanna
THE QUAIL'S EGG: A FOLKTALE
FROM SRI LANKA. Illus: Joanna
Broughton. Peter Bedrock, 1988. A quail
loses her egg and asks a mason for help.
The mason refuses so she seeks revenge
by asking the pig to trample the mason's
field. She then stirs up the other animals
to get the pig into action. Age: 3-5 years.

Burke, Eddie, & Garside, Anne
WATER IN THE GOURD AND OTHER
JAMAICAN FOLK STORIES. Illus:
Betty Anderson. Oxford: Oxford
University Press, 1979. Eight short stories
related to Jamaican culture. Although
each story is written in English, they
include Jamaican dialect for emphasis.
Age: 8 and older.

Dee, Ruby
A LIBERIAN FOLKTALE. Illus: Susan
Meddaugh. New York: Holt, Rinehart &
Winston, 1988. The antelope is the one to
figure out the riddle and win the contest to
marry the king's daughter proving that the
cleverest gets the prize. Age: 4-6 years.

de Paola, Tomie
ADELITA: A MEXICAN CINDERELLA
STORY. Illus: Tomie de Paola. New
York: G. P. Putnam's Sons, 2002. A
retelling of the Cinderella story with
Adelita as the mistreated and Esperanza,
a former cook and housekeeper as the one
who helps her get to the ball where the
falls in love with her.
Age: 6 and older.

de Paola, Tomie
THE MYSTERIOUS GIANT OF
BARLETTA. Illus: Tomie de Paola. New
York: Gryphon House, 1990. In this

retelling of an Italian folktale the people of Barletta are saved from invaders by a stone giant. Age: 3-8 years.

de Paola, Tomie
STREGA NONA. Illus: Tomie de Paola. New York: Scholastic, Inc., 1975. Strega Nona is a "grandma witch." When her assistant disobeys her, he is forced to learn a very important lesson. Age: 6-10 years.

Diakite, Baba Wague
THE HATSELLER AND THE MONKEYS: A WEST AFRICAN FOLKTALE (Retold). Illus: Baba Wague Diakite. New York: Scholastic Inc., 1999. A folktale from Mali, West Africa tells of a hatseller who learns an important lesson when his hats are stolen by a tree full of mischievous monkeys.
Age: 4 years and older.

Diakite, Baba Wague
THE HUNTERMAN AND THE CROCODILE: A WEST AFRICAN FOLKTALE (Retold). Illus: Baba Wague Diakite. New York: Scholastic Press, 1997. Donso, the Hunterman, learns from some animals and a tree how man needs to respect and live in harmony with nature. Age: 5 years and older.

Ginsburg, Mirra
THE CHINESE MIRROR. Illus: Margot Zemach. New York: Harcourt, Brace Jovanovich Publishers, 1988. A Korean villager returns from China with a strange object that shows people's faces. The wife, mother-in-law, father-in -law and neighbor become baffled, angry, and confused by the image they see in the mirror. Age: 5-10 years.

Haley, Gail E.
A STORY, A STORY. Illus: Gail E. Haley. New York: Aladdin books, 1970. All the stories once belonged to Nyame, the Story God. Ananse uses trickery, as usual, to buy the stories from Nyame. Age: 5-8 years.

Harris, Joel C.
JUMP ON OVER! THE ADVENTURES OF BRER RABBIT AND HIS FAMILY. Illus: Barry Moser. New York: Harcourt, 1989. This book contains five Brer Rabbit stories from the American South. In these stories Brer Rabbit, once again, attempts to out fox Brer Fox. Age: 4-6 years.

Ike, Jane & Zimmerman, Baruch
A JAPANESE FAIRY TALE. Illus: Pictures by Jane Ike. New York: Frederick Warner & Co., Inc., 1982. Tells how Kyoto learns that her husband had persuaded the gods to give him the ugliness and the deformity that was meant for her. Age 6-8 years.

Kimmel, Eric, A.
ANANSI AND THE MOSS COVERED ROCK. Illus: Janet Stevens. New York: Holiday House, 1988. An Ashanti tale in which Anansi finds a magic rock which will put people to sleep when they say certain words. He puts them to sleep and then robs them. However, he is outwitted by Little Lush Deer who has been watching the whole thing. Age: 6-10 years.

Kismaric, Carole (Adapted by)
THE RUMOR OF PAVEL AND PAALI: A UKRAINIAN FOLKTALE. Illus: Charles Mikolaycak. New York: Harper & Row, 1988. Two brothers make a

wager. The evil brother, Pavel initially wins but it is Paali who eventually becomes victor. Age: 8-10 years.

Lee, Jeanne M.
TOAD IS THE UNCLE OF HEAVEN. Illus: Jeanne M. Lee. New York: Gryphon House, 1990. Toad earns honor in this Vietnamese folktale. However, he must croak in order that rain will be sent from heaven. Age: 4-8 years.

Lewis, J. Patrick
THE TSAR AND THE AMAZING COW Illus.: Friso Henstra. New York: Dial Press, 1988. After suffering many hardships, two Russian peasants are helped by a cow who instructs them to drink her magic milk. They are then able to leave and become reunited with the three daughters they had. Age: 4-8 years.

Mann, Kenny
I AM NOT AFRAID: BASED ON A MASAI TALE. Illus. Richard Leonard and Alfredo Alcala. New York: Bantam Little Rooster Book, 1993. Tiplit shows his younger brother, Leyo, how to respect and show courage when challenged by the river, trees and other forces. Age: 6-10 years.

McDermott, Gerald
ARROW TO THE SUN: A PUEBLO INDIAN TALE. Illus. Gerald McDermott. New York: Puffin Books, 1974. A Pueblo boy searches to find his father. He is helped by the Arrow Maker who makes him into an arrow and sends him to the sun where he finds his father. He then returns to the earth. Age: 6- 8 years.

McKissack, Patricia
FLOSSIE AND THE FOX. Illus. Rachel Isadora. New York: Scholastic Inc., 1986. Flossie's grandmother asks her to take a basket of eggs to Miz Viola over at the McCutchen place. Flossie's challenge is to deliver the eggs safely from the sly fox. Age: 6-8 years.

McKissack, Patricia
MONKEY-MONKEY'S TRICK. BASED ON AN AFRICAN FOLKTALE. Illus: Paul Meisel. New York: Random House, 1988. Monkey-Monkey, who is full of tricks, refuses the tricky Hyena's help to build his house. However, Monkey-Monkey tricks Hyena into building his house. Age: 5-10 years.

McKissack, Patricia
NETTIE JO'S FRIENDS. Illus. New York: Alfred Knopf, 1986. Nettie Jo, an African-American, has to attend a wedding. As she searches for a needle to make a dress for her doll she meets and befriends many animals. Age: 4-9 years.

Morgan, Pierr
THE TURNIP: AN OLD RUSSIAN FOLKTALE. Illus: Pierr Morgan. New York: The Putnam & Grosset Group, 1996. Dedoushka's turnip grows to an enormous size. He is unable to uproot it from the ground so he gets help from family members and animals. Age: 4-10 years.

Mwalimu & Kennaway, Adrienne
AWFUL AARDVARK. Illus: Adrienne Kennaway. Boston: Little, Brown & Company, 1989. Aardvark, in this African tale, keeps the other animals awake at

night because of his loud snoring. Mongoose conspires with the other animals to get rid of Aardvark. Age: 6-8 years.

Nunes, Susan
TIDDALICK THE FROG. Illus: Ju-Hong Chen. New York: Atheneum, 1989. An Australian Aboriginal story about Tiddalick, who drinks all the water. Soon they get the frog to laugh and hence release the water. Age: 5-7 years.

Polacco, Patricia
BABUSHKA BABA YAGA. Illus: Patricia Polacco. New York: Penguin Putnam Books, 1993. To experience the joys of being a grandmother, Baba Yaga disguises herself as an old woman. Age: 6-8 years.

Polacco, Patricia
RECHENKA'S EGGS. Illus: Patricia Polacco. New York: The Putnam Grosset Group, 1988. The story, which is set in Russia tells how Rechenka breaks some of the eggs Babushka is painting for a contest. Rechenka then lays painted eggs to help Babushka win the prize. Age: 5-7 years.

Rohmer, Harriet
UNCLE NACHO'S HAT. Illus: Veg Reisberg. Children's Book Press, 1989. Nicaraguan Folktale. Uncle Nacho's niece gives him a new hat but he does not want to get rid of the old one. Age: 5-8 years.

San Souci, Robert
THE BOY AND THE GHOST. Illus: J. Brian Pinkney. New York: Simon & Schuster, 1989. Based on an older

Spanish version, the story tells of how a ghost rewards a little Southern African-American boy for his kindness. Age: 4-7 years.

San Souci, Robert
THE TALKING EGGS: A FOLKTALE FROM THE AMERICAN SOUTH. Illus: Jerry Pinkney. New York: Dial Press, 1989. A story about two sisters from the American South. One sister is mean and the other is kind. The disobedient sister is rewarded with magic eggs that contain snakes and vermin which shows that not all that glitters is gold. Age: 6-10 years.

Slobodkina, Esphyr
CAPS FOR SALE: A TALE OF A PEDDLER, SOME MONKEYS AND THEIR BUSINESS. Illus: Esphyr Slobodkina. New York: Harper Trophy 1968. The European version of a story about a cap peddler whose caps are stolen by some mischievous monkeys and how the peddler successfully retrieves the caps. Age: 3-8.

Walker, Barbara
A TREASURY OF TURKISH FOLKTALE FOR CHILDREN. Linnet Books/Shoestring, 1988. A collection of a variety of entertaining folktale. Age: 8 -10

Young, Ed
LON PO PO: A RED RIDING HOOD STORY FROM CHINA. Translated and illustrated by Ed Young. New York: Philomel Books, 1989. This is another version of the popular Red Riding Hood story with a Chinese motif. Age: 5-8 years.

FOOD

Paulsen, Gary
THE TORTILLA FACTORY. Paintings by Ruth Wright Paulsen. New York: Voyager Books, 1995. This cyclical story describes how the seed is planted in the black earth to the point when the crop is harvested and the tortilla, a Latino staple, is baked, delivered and served. Age: 4-10 years.

Soto, Gary
TOO MANY TAMALES. Illus. Ed Martinez New York: G. P. Putnam's Sons, 1993. Maria feels grown up helping to make tamales. She decides to try on her mother's ring which she later discovers is missing. Believing the ring is lost in the batter, Maria and her cousins decide to eat all the tamales. Age: 5-10 years.

FRIENDSHIP AND SHARING

Clifton, Lucille
EVERETT ANDERSON'S FRIEND. Illus: Ann Grifalconi. New York: Holt, Rinehart & Winston, 1976. Everett Anderson, an African-American boy, is disappointed that the new neighbors consist of a mother and daughter. He later learns that they are good neighbors and that Maria, plus his two male friends, make a good foursome. Age: 5-8 years.

Clifton, Lucille
MY FRIEND JACOB. Illus: Thomas DiGrazia. New York: E.P. Dutton, 1980. Jacob, the White boy next door, is developmentally delayed. He and Sammy, an African-American, become best friends and together they help each other. Age: 3-8 years.

Clifton, Lucille
ONE OF THE PROBLEMS OF EVERETT ANDERSON. Illus: Ann Grifalconi. New York: Henry Holt & Co., 2001. Everett recognizes a problem when one of his friends constantly comes to school with bruises and claims he is clumsy. Age: 5-8 years.

Clifton, Lucille
THREE WISHES. Illus: Michael Hays. New York: Bantam Doubleday Dell publishing Group Inc., 1992. Zenobia, an African American girl believes in good luck. She finds a good luck penny and makes three wishes one of which restores her friendship with her best friend. Age: 7-10 years.

Havill, Juanita
JAMAICA AND BRIANNA. Illus: Anne Sibley O'Brien. New York: Houghton Mifflin Co. 1993. After Brianna's comments, Jamaica no longer wants to wear her brother's hand-me-down boy boots. Age: 5-8 years.

Havill, Juanita
JAMAICA'S FIND. Illus: O'Brien, Anne Sibley. New York: Gryphon House, 1990. Jamaica, a young African-American girl, takes home a toy dog she finds in the park. She is forced to return the toy and ends up finding not only the owner but also a friend. Age: 3-7 years.

Havill, Juanita
JAMAICA TAG-ALONG. Illus: Anne Sibley O'Brien. New York: Houghton, 1989. Ossie, an older African American

child, refuses to allow little sister, Jamaica, to play basketball with him. Jamaica soon finds out what it is like to be the big child. Age: 4-6 years.

Jin, Sarunna
MY FIRST AMERICAN FRIEND. Illus: Shirley V. Beckes. New York: Raintree Steck-Vaughn Publishers, 1992. A little girl who has just migrated to the United States does not speak English and, as a result, experiences many difficulties. Age: 6 years and older.

Jones, Rebecca, C.
MATTHEW AND TILLY. Illus: Beth Peck. New York: Dutton Children's Books, 1991. Two friends, one black and one white, had a falling out then realize that their friendship is very important. Age: 6 and older.

Keats, Ezra Jack
A LETTER TO AMY. Illus: Ezra Jack Keats. New York: Harper & Row Publishers, 1974. In this story about some Hispanic children, Peter is embarrassed when he bumps into Amy on his way to mail her an invitation to his birthday party.
Age: 3-8 years.

Keats, Ezra Jack
LOUIE. Illus: Ezra Jack Keats. New York: Greenwillow Books, 1975. Some Hispanic children decide to put on a puppet show. Louie, who would not speak, begins to interact with a puppet during the show. Susie and Roberto, then decide to give the puppet to Louie as a surprise gift. Age: 3-8 years.

Keats, Ezra Jack
PET SHOW. Illus: Ezra Jack Keats. New York: Aladdin Books, 1987. A Pet Show is about to take place in this Hispanic neighborhood but Archie's cat has disappeared. Age:3-8 years.

Kline, Suzy
GREEN ENVY. Illus: Frank Remkiewicz. New York: Scholastic, Inc., 1993. A little girl in Song Lee's class is jealous because Song Lee has a lot of friends and a secret she will not share. Soon the girl finds out that Song Lee is indeed a very nice person. Age: 6-10.

Lessac, Frane
MY LITTLE ISLAND. Illus. New York: Gryphon House, 1990. A little boy decides to return home to the Caribbean where he also takes his friend. Age: 4-8 years.

Uchida, Yoshiko
THE BRACELET. Illus: Joanna Yardley. New York: The Putnam and Grosset Group, 1993. Emi, a Japanese-American girl, is being sent with her family to an internment camp. She is given a bracelet by her best friend Laurie. She loses the bracelet but soon realizes she does not need it to remember her friend. Age: 5 and older.

GOOD LUCK/GOOD FORTUNE

Alexander, Lloyd
THE FORTUNE TELLERS. Illus. Trina Schart Hyman. New York: Dutton Children's Books, 1992. A carpenter, in the Cameroons, went to a fortune-teller to learn what his life will be like. After

wonderful predictions there is a funny turn of events. The fortune-teller disappears and the predictions come through. Age: 6-8 years.

GOOD OVERCOMES EVIL

Armstrong, Jennifer.
CHIN YU MIN AND THE GINGER CAT. Illus: Mary Grandpre. New York: Crown Publishers, Inc., 1993. Chin Yu Min, a Chinese widow, learns about the joy of giving and friendship through a ginger cat that wandered into her life. Age: 5-8 years.

Climo, Shirley
THE KOREAN CINDERELLA. Illus. Ruth Heller. New York: Harper Collins, 1993. Pear Blossom is mistreated by her stepmother and stepsister. One day, as she is running away from the Magistrate, she loses her sandal. He searches for her, finds her and marries her. Age: 5-8 years.

Louie, Ai-Ling.
YEH-SHEN: A CINDERELLA STORY FROM CHINA. Illus: Ed Young. New York: Philomel Books, 1982. Yeh-Shen, a Chinese orphan, is abused by her stepmother. She is helped by her fairy godmother to attend a fancy ball. She loses her slipper which the king finds and searches for the owner. Age:6 and older.

Martin, Rafe
THE ROUGH FACE GIRL: ALGONQUIN INDIAN CINDERELLA STORY. Illus. David Shannon. New York: Scholastic, Inc., 1992. Only the woman capable of seeing the Invisible Being will be able to marry him. In true Cinderella style, the mistreated youngest sister from a family, in a village close by, is the one. Age 5-7.

Perrault, Charles (translated by Marcia Brown)
CINDERELLA OR THE LITTLE GLASS SLIPPER. Illus: Marcia Brown. New York: Charles Scribner's Sons, 1954. Translated from French, this story tells how Cinderella after being mistreated by her step-mother and step-sisters is dressed for the ball by her fairy godmother. Cinderella loses her glass slipper and is pursued by the prince who finds her and marries her. Age: 5-8 years.

San Souci, Robert D.
CENDRILLON: CARIBBEAN CINDERELLA. Illus: Brian Pinkney. New York: Simon & Schuster, 1998. Cinderella story with a Caribbean flare. The story is told by Cendrillon's godmother who is Cendrillon's chaperone to the ball where she meets Monsieur Thibault's son. Age: 5-10 years.

Steptoe, John
MUFARO'S BEAUTIFUL DAUGHTERS: AN AFRICAN TALE. Illus. Paintings by John Steptoe. New York: Gryphon House, 1990. This is an African fable about two sisters. One sister is kind and the other is ill-tempered. In the long run, goodness overcomes arrogance. Age: 5-10 years.

HELPING OTHERS

Aardema Verna
BRINGING THE RAIN TO KAPITI PLAIN. Illus: Beatriz Vidal. New York: The Dial Press, 1981. Ki-Pat using a

feather dropped by an eagle makes an arrow which he uses to shoot through the clouds and break the drought on Kapiti Plain in Africa. Age: 6-8 years.

Appiah, Sonia
AMOKO AND THE EFUA BEAR. Illus: Carol Easmon. New York: Macmillan, 1989. The story takes place in West Africa. Amoko's aunt brings her a new drum and Amoko is excited until the dogs rip her favorite bear. She will not be appeased until the bear is mended. Age: 4-7 years.

Bang, Molly
THE PAPER CRANE. Illus: Molly Bang. New York: Green Willow Books, 1985. A Japanese-American story about a restaurant owner who began to lose business because of the new highway. A poor stranger, unable to pay, gives the owner a paper crane which helps to improve business. Age: 6-8 years.

de Paola, Tomie
JINGLE THE CHRISTMAS CLOWN. Illus: Tomie de Paola. New York: Scholastic Inc., 1992. Every year the circus Il Circo Picolo, goes to the big city but stops at the village first. This year, however, the villagers have no money for the circus. Jingle and his animal friends have an idea so as not to disappoint the villagers. Age: 5-10 years.

Fleming, Candace
GABRIELLA'S SONG. Illus: Giselle Potter. New York: Atheneum Books for Young Readers, 1997. As Gabriella walks along the streets of Venice, the street sounds become a song to her ear. Others pick up the song and soon it is written into a symphony by an accomplished composer. Age: 5-10 years.

Nikly, Michelle
THE EMPEROR'S PLUM TREE. Illus: Michelle Nikly. New York: Green Willow Books, The Japanese Emperor's plum tree died. The Emperor summoned Ukiyo to bring him his plum tree as a replacement. However, he later changed his mind. Age: 7-9 years.

Polacco, Patricia
CHICKEN SUNDAY. Illus: Patricia Polacco. New York: Scholastic Inc., 1992. The author recounts the friendship between her, Winston and Stewart and the close relationship with Miss Eula Mae, the boys' African American grandmother. The children want to buy Miss Eula a hat she admires but run into some problems. Age: 7-10 years.

Surat, Michelle Maria
ANGEL CHILD, DRAGON CHILD. Illus: Vo-Dinh Mai. New York: Scholastic, Inc., 1983. A young Vietnamese girl is not enjoying school in the United States. Then the boy who has been taunting her the most is the one who finds a way to help raise money to get her mother to migrate to the United States. Age: 6 years and older.

Yolen, Jane
RAISING YODER'S BARN. Illus: Bernie Fuchs. New York: Little Brown and Co., 1998. An Amish family's farm burns down and a young member, the narrator, wants very much to help rebuild the farm.
Age: 7-10 years.

HISTORY -- PEOPLE/PLACES

Adler, David A.
JACKIE ROBINSON: HE WAS THE FIRST. Illus: Robert Casilla. New York: Holiday House, 1989. A biography with black and white pictures tracing the career of Jackie Robinson, an African American. Age: 8 years and up.

Bendick, Jeanne
EGYPTIAN TOMBS. Illus. (with photographs). London: Franklin Watts, 1989. This book provides a description of Egyptian views about preparation for burial, the after life and their famous tombs. Age: 8 years and older.

Cha, Dia
DIA'S STORY CLOTH: THE HMONG PEOPLE'S JOURNEY OF FREEDOM. Illus: Stitched by Chue and Nhia Thao Cha. New York: Lee and Low Books, Inc., 1996. The life of the Hmong is told in a story cloth. This includes their time in Laos to the upheaval and ultimate refugee status of some to various countries. Age:7 years and older.

Fisher, Leonard Everett
THE WAILING WALL. Illus: Leonard Fisher. New York: Macmillan, 1989. An account of Jewish history, the sites owned by the Jews and why they are important. Age: 8 years and older.

Meyer, Carolyn
A VOICE FROM JAPAN: AN OUTSIDER LOOKS IN. Illus: Carolyn Meyer. New York: Gulliver/ Harcourt, 1988. A depiction of Japan is given through pictures and the description

provided by visitors. Age:7 years and older.

Morimoto, Junko
MY HIROSHIMA. Illus: Illustrations and photographs. New York: Puffin Books, 1987. After many years the author returns to Hiroshima. The story is about her life before and after the bombing Hiroshima. Age: 7 years and older.

HOLIDAYS/CELEBRATIONS

Adler, David
A PICTURE BOOK OF JEWISH HOLIDAYS. Illus. Linda Heller. New York: Holiday House, 1981. Each page of this book describes a Jewish holiday. Why each holiday is important is also discussed. Ages: 6-8 years.

Ancona, George
PABLO REMEMBERS: THE FIESTA OF THE DAY OF THE DEAD. Illus: George Ancona. New York: Lothrop, Lee & Shepard Books, 1993. Pedro, a Mexican boy describes what takes place as Mexicans celebrate their dead relatives. Age: 6-9 years

Behrens, J.
POW WOW: FESTIVALS AND HOLIDAYS. Illus: J. Behrens. Chicago, Ill: Children's Press, 1983. Different types of festivals and holidays are described. Age: 6 years and older.

Burden-Patmon, Denise & Jones, Kathryn
CARNIVAL. Illus: Reynold Ruffins. New York: Modern Curriculum Press, Inc. 1992. A little girl has moved from

Trinidad to Brooklyn to live with relatives. She is unhappy because she misses the Carnival. Age: 7-10 years.

Burden- Patman, Denise
IMANI'S GIFT AT KWANZAA.. Illus: Floyd Cooper. New York: Simon and Schuster, 1992. Imani, a little African American girl, does not like her young neighbor but decides to be nice as she prepares for Kwanzaa with her grandmother. Age: 6-10

Bunting, Eve
HOW MANY DAYS TO AMERICA? A THANKSGIVING STORY. Illus: Beth Peck. New York: Clarion Books, 1985. A family forced to leave their home in the Caribbean travel by boat to the United States. After having some problems with immigration, they arrive in time for Thanksgiving. Age: 5-10 years.

Charles, Freda
THE MYSTERY OF THE MISSING CHALAH. Illus: Lil Goldstein. New York: Jonathan David Publishers, 1959. A young girl is considered too young to participate in the Jewish celebrations but does her part by finding the missing Chalah. Age: 5-8.

Chinn, Karen
SAM AND THE LUCKY MONEY. Illus: Cornelius Van Wright and Ying-Hwa Hu. New York: Lee and Low Books, 1995. Sam receives four dollars in lucky money as his Chinese New Year gift. This year he has permission to spend it and decides it is not enough until he realizes there are others who have less. Age: 4 and older.

Chocolate, Deborah M. Newton
MY FIRST KWANZAA BOOK. Illus: Cal Massey. New York: Scholastic Inc., 1992. This story gives a brief description of what takes place during the seven days of Kwanzaa, an African American holiday. Swahili terms and their meaning are provided. Age: 5 and older.

Delacre, Lulu
LAS NAVIDADES: POPULAR CHRISTMAS SONGS FROM LATIN, AMERICA. Illus: Lulu Delacre. New York: Scholastic Inc., 1990. This book contains Christmas songs from various parts of Latin America. The songs are in both Spanish and English with an explanation of their origin. Age: 10 and older.

Ehrlich, Amy.
THE STORY OF HANUKKAH. Paintings by Ori Sherman. New York: Dial Books, 1989. This story describes early in history when the Jews fought against Antiochus and his armies. To celebrate their victory they light a lamp which burns for eight days. This is the beginning of the burning of the lights of Hanukkah. Age: 5 years and older.

Ford, Juwanda
K IS FOR KWANZAA. Illus: Ken Wilson Max. New York: Scholastic, Inc., 1997. The meaning of Kwanzaa is given through the alphabet. Age: 5 and older.

Gardeski, Christina Mia
DIVALI. Photographs, Caroline Anderson. New York: Children's Press, 2001. The story describes what takes place during the Hindu celebration. Age: 6-10.

Gilmore, Rachna
LIGHTS FOR GITA. Illus: Alice Priestly. Gardner, Maine: Tilbury House Publishers, 1994. Gita, an East Indian girl, is angry and upset because she fears the Duvali celebration is ruined. It is gloomy and cold here in the United States. However, things soon take a different turn. Age 5-10 years.

Gold, Margery
HAPPY HANUKKAH. Illus: John Speirs. New York: Western Publishing Co., Inc. This story describes why Hanukkah is celebration and what takes place during the celebration. Age: 6-10 years.

Groner, Judye & Wikler, Madeline
ALL ABOUT HANUKKAH. Illus: Rosalyn Schanzer. New York: Gryphon House, 1990. The story of Hanukkah is told through songs and games. Illustrations are used to explain the Lighting of the Candles and the Blessing. Age: 4-8 years.

Hayes, Sarah
HAPPY CHRISTMAS, GEMMA. Illus: Jan Ormerod. New York: Gryphon House, 1990. It is Gemma's first Christmas, in this African-American household. The story describes the part that Gemma plays in this traditional celebration. Age: 3-6 years.

Jennings, Paula
STRAWBERRY THANKSGIVING. Illus. Ramona Peters. New York: Modern Curriculum Press, 1992. In this Native American story, Adam is excited as he and his family get ready to go to the reservation for the Strawberry celebration. Age: 5-8 years.

Jimenez, Francisco
THE CHRISTMAS GIFT. New York: Houghton Mifflin, 2000. A little Mexican boy has to move again as his family looks for work. The boy worries he may not get the gift he wants. Age: 5-8 yeas.

Kimmel, Eric
HERSHEL AND THE HANUKKAH GOBLINS. Illus. Trina Schart Hyman. New York: Holiday House, 1989. The villagers have decided not to celebrate Hanukkah because they are afraid of the goblins in the Synagogue. Hershel is not from the village and so he plans to outwit the goblins for the eight nights of Hanukkah. Age: 5-8 years.

Kimmel, Eric
THE CHANUKAH GUEST. Illus. Giora Carmi. New York: Scholastic Inc., 1988. Bubba Brayna, who doesn't see very well, prepares a Chanukah feast. On the first night she feeds her guest and later realizes her mistake when the invited guests arrive. Age: 5-8 years.

Kleven, Elisa
HOORAY, A PINATA! Illus: Elisa Kleven. New York: Dutton Children's Books, 1996. A young Hispanic girl chooses a dog pinata for her birthday. However, she does not want to break - she wants to keep it as a pet. Age: 3 and older.

Kroll, Virginia
A CARP FOR KIMIKO. Illus: Katherine Roundtree. New York: Charlesbridge Publishing, 1993. Flying a carp kite for Children's Day is a Japanese tradition reserved for boys. Kimiko feels left out so her parents find a way to appease her. Age: 4-10 years.

Manushkin, Fran
THE MATZAH THAT PAPA BROUGHT HOME. Illus: Ned Bittinger. New York: Scholastic Inc., 1997. This story is about Passover which begins with the Matzah that the father brings home. Age: 4 and older.

Pinkney, Andrea D.
SEVEN CANDLES FOR KWANZAA. Illus: Brian Pinkey. New York: Scholastic Inc., 1993. The seven days of Kwanzaa with the principles are described. Swahili terms and their pronunciation are also given. Age: 5 and older.

Polacco, Patricia
THE TREES OF THE DANCING GOATS. Illus: Patricia Polacco. New York: Simon and Schuster, 1996. A Jewish family help their Christian, bedridden neighbors decorate for Christmas. Age: 5 and older.

Politi, Leo
MR. FONG'S TOY SHOP. Illus. Leo Politi. New York: Charles Scribner's Sons, 1978. Some children become interested in the toys and puppetry skills of Mr. Fong, a Chinese American, who owns a toyshop. For the Moon Festival, the children help Mr. Fong entertain with a puppet shoe. Age: 6-8 years.

Porter, A. P.
KWANZAA. Illus. Janice Porter. Minneapolis: Carolrhoda Books, Inc., 1991. The story of Kwanzaa, an African-American celebration, is explained. Swahili terms and their meaning for various parts of the celebration are also explained. Age: 4-8 years.

Rattigan, Jama Kim
DUMPLING SOUP. Illus: Lillian Hsu-Flanders. New York: Little, Brown and Company, 1993. This year Marisa, a seven year-old Hawaiian girl is allowed to help make dumplings for the New Year celebration. Age: 5 and older.

Say, Allen
TREE OF CRANES. Illus. Boston: Houghton Mifflin Company, 1991. A Japanese mother decides to combine two cultures so her son can celebrate his first Christmas. Age 3-8 years.

Daniel Pennington
ITSE SELU. Illus: Don Stewart. New York: Charlesbridge Co. A young Cherokee boy and his family get ready for the annual four-day Itse Selu festival. Age: 4 and older.

Steffy, Jan
THE SCHOOL PICNIC. Illus: Denny Bond. New York: New York: Gryphon House, 1990. A group of Amish children in Lancaster County decide to have a picnic to celebrate the last day of school. Age: 5-8 years.

Suyenaga, Ruth, Young, Sook Kim & Young, Mi Pak.
KOREAN CHILDREN'S DAY. Illus: Nani Kyong-Nan. New York: Modern Curriculum Press, 1992. A Korean boys invites his friend to his Saturday Korean class. The story describes Korean traditions such as foods eaten, different dances. Age: 7-10 years.

"Trosclair" Edited by Howard Jacobs. CAJUN NIGHT BEFORE CHRISTMAS. Illus. James Rice. Louisiana: Pelican Publishing Co., 1988. This tale, written in Cajun dialect, is a description of Christmas Eve night as Santa Claus makes his way across the bayou in Louisiana to deliver gifts. Age: 6-10.

Urrutia, Maria Christina
CINCO DE MAYO: YESTERDAY AND TODAY. Illus: Maria Christina Urrutia and Rebecca Orozco. New York: Greenwood Books Ltd./Douglas and McIntyre, 1999. Mexico's fight for independence from the French is the summary of the story. Age: 8 and older.

IMAGINATION AND FANTASY

Adoff, Arnold
FLAMBOYAN. Illus. Karen Barbour. New York: Harcourt Brace, 1988. Told in poetic form, this story is about Flamboyan, a little girl in the Caribbean. She dreams of flying high in the sky. Age: 5-8 years.

Gerstein, Mordecai
THE MOUNTAINS OF TIBET. Illus. Mordecai Gerstein. New York: Harper Row, 1987. A little boy who dies before fulfilling his dreams of visiting far away places is reincarnated. Age: 5-7 years.

Greenfield, Eloise
AFRICA DREAM. Illus: Carole Byard. New York: The John Day Company, 1977. A young African-American girl dreams that she is in Africa where she meets her ancestors and enjoys the African lifestyle and food. Age: 3-6 years.

Greenfield, Eloise
ME AND NESSIE. Illus. Moneta Barnett. New York: Harper Trophy, 1975. Janell, an African American girl, has a best friend Nessie but only she can see Nessie. When Aunt Bea visits, Nessie appears and is quite mischievous. Age: 4-8 years.

Isadora, Rachel
BEN'S TRUMPET. Illus: Rachel Isadora. New York: Scholastic Inc., 1979. Ben, an African-American boy, is so fascinated with the trumpet that he sometimes plays his pretend trumpet. Then one day one of the musicians decides to show Ben how to play the trumpet. Age: 5-8 years.

Keats, Ezra Jack
REGARDS TO THE MAN IN THE MOON. Illus. Ezra jack Keats. New York: Macmillan Publishing Company, 1981. Louie is sad because the children tease him saying his father is a junk man. His father advises him to use his imagination which he does. The other children then begin to use their imagination. Age: 5-8 years.

Lobel, Arnold
MING LO MOVES THE MOUNTAIN. Illus. Arnold Lobel. Scholastic Inc., New York, 1982. Ming Lo and his wife live at the bottom of the mountain. They are unhappy there and seek the advise of the wise man. After several attempts, the wise man gives a full-proof, hilarious solution. Age:5-8 years.

McKissack, Patricia
A MILLION FISH .....MORE OR LESS. Illus. Dena Schutzer. New York: Alfred Knopf, 1992. Hugh Thomas goes fishing on the bayou Clapateaux where he meets

Papa Daddy and Elder Abbayon. After hearing their yarn about events they experienced, Hugh Thomas also exaggerates his fishing experience on his return from the Bayou. Age: 6-8 years.

McKissack, Patricia
MIRANDY AND BROTHER WIND. Illus: Jerry Pinkney. New York: Alfred Knopf, 1988. Mirandy, an African-American girl, wants the wind as her partner in the walking contest but the wind constantly eludes her. With clumsy Ezel as her partner she is able to win the contest along with the wind which she has captured. Age: 5-8 years.

Mendez, Phil
THE BLACK SNOWMAN. Illus: Carole Byard. New York: Scholastic Inc., 1989. Two Black children make a snowman. The snowman comes to life and tells them about their heritage. Age: 5-8 years.

Rawlins, Donna
DIGGING TO CHINA. Illus: Donna Rawlins. New York: Orchard Press, 1989. For the gardener's birthday Alexis decides to dig a hole to China. When she presents the `gift' two Chinese children emerge. Age: 5-8 years.

Ringgold, Faith
TAR BEACH. Illus. Faith Ringgold. New York: Scholastic Inc., 1991. An African-American girl describes what it is like the many nights she and her family, along with some neighbors, spend on Tar Beach (the rooftop). Age: 6-10 years.

Walter, Mildred Pitts
TY'S ONE-MAN BAND. Illus. Margot Tomez. New York: Scholastic Inc., 1980.

While lying down by the pond, on a hot summer day, Ty meets a man with one leg who claims to be a musician. Age: 5-8 years.

INTERGENERATIONAL RELATIONSHIPS

Ackerman, Karen
SONG AND DANCE MAN. Illus. Stephen Gammell. New York: Scholastic inc., 1988. Some young children are entertained in their grandfather's attic by the grandfather who once was a vaudeville performer. Age: 6-8 years..

Allen, Thomas B.
ON GRANDDADDY'S FARM. Illus. New York: Gryphon House, 1990. This story is about an African-American man's life, as a boy, on his grandfather's farm in the 1930s. Age: 4-8 years.

Bradman, Tony
WAIT AND SEE. Illus: Eileen Browne. Oxford: Franklin Watts, 1988. An interracial English girl describes her experiences on the day she goes to various stores with her mother in a mixed neighborhood. Age: 5-7 years.

Brisson, Pat
THE SUMMER MY FATHER WAS TEN. Illus: Andrea Shine. Pennsylvania: Boyds Mills Press, 1998. A young girl recounts a story told to her by her father. When he was ten he and his friends thoughtlessly destroyed an Italian neighbor's garden. This leads to a long term relationship with the man. Age: 6 and older.

Buckley, Helen. E.
GRANDFATHER AND I. Illus. Jan
Ormerod. New York: Harper Collins,
1994. A little African-American boy
describes how other people are always in
a hurry but he and his grandfather stop
and look as long as they like. Age:3-6.

Buckley, Helen, E.
GRANDMOTHER AND I. Illus: Jan
Ormerod. New York: Scholastic, Inc.,
1994. A little African American girl tells
how important grandmothers are. They
braid your hair and let you sit on their laps
as they read to you. Age: 3-6 years.

Bunting, Eve
A DAY'S WORK. Illus: Ronald Himler.
New York: Clarion Books, 1994.
Francisco, a little Mexican boy who is
bilingual, lies in order to help his Abuelo
get a job. He soon learns there are
consequences for such behavior. Age :5-
10 years.

Burrowes, Adjoa J.
GRANDMA'S PURPLE FLOWERS.
Illus: Adjoa J. Burrowes. New York: Lee
and Low Books, 2000. When a little
African American girl's grandmother dies
she realizes that everything has a season.
She cherishes her grandmother's memory
through the purple flowers they both love.
Age: 6 and older.

Cameron, Ann
THE MOST BEAUTIFUL PLACE IN
THE WORLD. Illus: Thomas B. New
York: Alfred Knopf, 1988. Juan, a
Guatemalan boy, who was abandoned by
his father is later left with his
grandmother when his mother remarries.
Through love and trust for his

grandmother, he learns to adjust to living
without his mother. Age: 8 years and
older.

Castaneda, Omar S.
ABUELA'S WEAVE. Illus: Enrique O.
Sanchez. New York: Lee and Low Books,
Inc., 1993. A Guatemalan grandmother
decides to weave her artifacts in the
traditional way. However she fears
commercial goods will do better than hers
at the market. Age: 5-8.

Cech, John
MY GRANDMOTHER'S JOURNEY.
Illus: Sharon McGinley-Nally. New York:
Aladdin Paperbacks, 1991. A Russian
grandmother shares with her
granddaughter her story of trials and
survival during and after the Russian
Revolution. Age: 8 and older.

Cheng, Andrea
GRANDFATHER COUNTS. Illus: Angie
Zhang. New York: Lee and Low Books,
2000. Helen's grandfather is coming from
China to live with her family but he only
speaks Chinese and she only speaks
English. Soon they learn to communicate
with each other. Age: 6-8 years.

Choi, Sook Nyul
HALMONI AND THE PICNIC. Illus:
Karen M. Duggan. Boston: Houghton
Mifflin Co., 1993. Yunmi, a little Korean
girl, invites her Halmoni (grandmother)
to her class picnic. While at the picnic the
children learn some things about Korean
cultures. Age: 4 and older.

Clifton, Lucille
THE LUCKY STONE. Illus: Dale
Payson. New York: Delacorte Press,

1979. The story is about Sweet Baby Tee, an African American girl, her grandmother and a lucky stone. Each chapter describes a different part of their lives and the different ways in which the stone brings luck. Age: 8-10 years.

Cowley, Joy
BIG MOON TORTILLA. Illus: Dyanne Strongbow. New York: Caroline House Publishers, 1998. A young girl runs into a series of "problems." Distressed she goes to her grandmother who provides her with some alternatives. Age: 7 and older.

Daly, Niki
NOT SO FAST SONGOLOLO. Illus. Niki Daly. New York: Gryphon House, 1990. A little South African boy, Malusi, spends a day in the city with his grandmother. The day becomes more special when he receives a new pair of red tackies. Age: 4-9 years.

Dorros, Arthur
ABUELA. Illus: Elisa Kleven. New York: Dutton Children's Books, 1991. As a young Hispanic girl and her grandmother travel on a city bus the girl dreams of flying over New York city. Age: 5 and older.

de Paola, Tomie
STREGA NONA: HER STORY. Illus: Tomie de Paola. New York: Puffin Books, 1996. Since Nona's birth Grandma Concetta has been teaching her to be a very good Strega. Eventually, Grandma Concetta leaves Nona the magic pot. Age: 7 and older.

Flournoy, Valerie
THE PATCHWORK QUILT. Illus: Jerry Pinkney. New York: Dial Books for Young Readers, 1985. A little African American girl learns the importance of preserving family memories and values through quilt making. Age: 5 and older.

Fox, Mem
SOPHIE. Illus: Aminah Brenda Lynn Robinson. New York: Harcourt Brace and Co., 1994. Sophie, an African-American girl loved her grandfather. Then grandfather is no more. However, the emptiness she feels is short lived. Age: 3 and older.

Greenfield, Eloise
GRANDPA'S FACE. Illus: Floyd Cooper. New York: Philomel Books, 1988. Tamica, a little African American girl, learns that even though her grandfather may display many "faces", his love for her is unconditional. Age: 4-7 years

Grifalconi, Ann
THE VILLAGE OF ROUND AND SQUARE HOUSES. Illus: Ann Grifalconi. Boston: Little Brown and Company, 1986. After a village in To, West Central Africa, was destroyed by a volcano, the villagers rebuild with women in round and men in square houses. Age: 5- 10 years.

Johnson, Angela
WHEN I AM OLD WITH YOU. Illus: David Soman. New York: Barton Press, Inc., 1990. A small boy describes what life is like with his grandfather. Age: 6 and older.

Keans-Douglas, Richardo
GRANDPA'S VISIT. Illus: Frances Clancy. New York: Annick Press (U. S.) Ltd., 1996. Grandpa visits unexpectedly but both parents work two jobs and Jeremy, his grandson, is only interested in television and video games. Then there is a power failure and things change. Age: 4-10 years.

Keats, Ezra Jack
APT. 3. Illus. Ezra Jack Keats. New York: Macmillan Publishing Co., 1971.Two brothers decide to search their apartment building to locate the harmonic music. They get a surprise when they find the musician. Age: 4 - 8 years.

Keller, Holly
GRANDFATHER'S DREAM. Illus: Holly Keller. New York: Greenwillow Books, 1994. A Vietnamese grandfather dreams that the sarus cranes will return now that the Vietnam war is over. However, some of the villagers would rather use the land to plant rice. Age 5-9 years.

MacLachlan, Patricia
THROUGH GRANDPA'S EYES. Illus. Deborah Kogan Ray. New York: Harper Trophy Publishers, 1980. John enjoys spending time at his grandfather's house because his grandfather, who is blind, helps him to see in different ways Age:3-10 years.

Markel, Michelle
GRACIAS ROSA. Illus: Diane Patterson. New York: Albert Whitman and Co. 1995. A strong bond develops between a young girl and her Guatemalan babysitter. Age: 6-10.

Martin, Bill, Jr., & Archambault, John
KNOTS ON A COUNTING ROPE. Illus. Ted Rand. New York: Scholastic Inc., 1987. A Native American grandfather shares with his grandson the day of the grandson's birth and the naming ceremony. Each time the grandfather tells the story, a knot is tied on the rope. Age: 4- 10 years.

Michelson, Richard
TOO YOUNG FOR YIDDISH. Illus: Neil Waldman. New York: Charlesbridge Publishing, 2002. A young Jewish boy's grandfather moves in with the family. He speaks Yiddish but will not teach his grandson until years later when he has to go to a nursing home. Age: 6-10.

Mower, N.
I VISIT MY TUTU AND GRANDMA. Illus. N. Mower. Pacifica, Kailua, Hawaii 1984. A little Hawaiian child, who is White, learns about the culture of each of her grandmothers Age: 5-8 years.

Ness, Evaline
JOSEFINA FEBRUARY. Illus: Evaline Ness. New York: Charles Scribner's Sons, 1963. This is a Haitian story about Josefina who wants to buy her grandfather a pair of real leather boots for his birthday. However, she is distracted on her way to the market and arrives when it is closed. Age: 8 -10 years.

Nicolai, Margaret
KITAQ GOES ICE SKATING. Illus: David Rubin. Alaska Nortwest Books, 1998. A six year old Yup'ik Eskimo boy learns about responsibility when he spends the day ice fishing with his grandfather. Age 3 and older.

Oliviero, Jamie
SOM SEE AND THE MAGIC ELEPHANT. Illus: Jo Anne Kelly. New York: Hyperion Books for Children, 1995. In this tale from Thailand, Pa Nang is about to die. Som See wants to grant her great-aunt's last wish to touch Chang, the great white elephant, for good luck. Age: 7-10 years.

Pak, Soyung
DEAR JUNO. Illus: Susan K. Hartung. New York: Puffin Books, 1999. Juno, a little Korean boy convinces his parents that he can read the letter he receives from his grandmother in Seoul. He responds to the letter in pictures. Age: 5 - 9 years.

Polacco, Patricia
BABUSHKA'S DOLL. Illus. Patricia Polacco. New York: Aladdin Paperbacks, 1995. Natasha is a very demanding girl. Her Babushka decides to teach Natasha a lesson by having her childhood doll come to life and makes unreasonable demands on Natasha. Age: 5-10 years.

Polacco, P.
MRS. KATZ AND TUSH. Illus: Patricia Polacco. New York: Bantam, Doubleday Dell Publishing. 1992. Larnel knew Mrs. Katz was lonely so he gives her a cat. But Mrs. Katz will only take the cat if Larnel helps take care of it. Through this arrangement, they get to know each other and realize they have much in common. Age: 4-10 years.

Pomerantz, Charlotte
THE CHALK DOLL. Illus: Frane Lessac. New York: Gryphon House, 1990. A Jamaican mother describes to her daughter how she managed to use her imagination with home-made play items because her mother could not afford to buy her a "chalk" doll. Age: 4-8 years.

Rylant, Cynthia
WHEN I WAS YOUNG IN THE MOUNTAINS. Illus. Diane Goode. New York: E. P. Dutton, 1982. Appalachian life is described by a little boy who, with his sister, is spending time with their grandparents. Age 6-10 years.

Sakai, Kimiko
SACHIKO MEANS HAPPINESS. Illus: Tomie Arai. New York: Children's Book Press, 1990. Sachiko was named after her grandmother who had limited abilities. At first Sachiko did not understand but when she did she bonded strongly with her grandmother. Age: 6 and older.

Sisulu, Elinor Batezat
THE DAY GOGO WENT TO VOTE. Illus. Sharon Wilson. Boston: Little, Brown and Company, 1996. For the first time in history black South Africans are allowed to vote. Six year-old Themb accompanies her great grandmother who is determined to exercise her right to vote. Age: 5-10 years.

Taulbert, Clifton
LITTLE CLIFF AND THE PORCH PEOPLE. Illus: E. B. Lewis. New York: Dial books for young readers, 1999. Little Cliff, an African American boy, goes to Mississippi to spend the summer with his grandparents. Many of the residents need assistance with to do things so Little Cliff helps them as well as his grandparents. Age:7 and older.

Taulbert, Clifton
LITTLE CLIFF'S FIRST DAY OF SCHOOL. Illus: E. B. Lewis. New York: Puffin Books, 2001. Little Cliff does not want to go to school where it is all work. However, when his grandmother walks with him to school he sees it can be fun. Age: 4-8 years.

Tompert, Ann
GRANDFATHER TANG'S STORY. Illus: Robert Andrew Parker. New York: Crown Publishers, Inc., 1990. A little Chinese girl likes to listen to stories and her grandfather likes to tell them so they develop a really good relationship. Age: 5 and older.

Tsuhakiyama, Margaret Holloway
MEI-MEI LOVES THE MORNING. Illus: Cornelius Von Wright & Ying-Hwa Hu. New York: Albert Whitman and Co., 1999. Mei-Mei loves to spend the morning with her grandfather. They go to the park, do Tai-Chi and then eat breakfast together. Age:3-8 years.

Wallace, Ian
CHIN CHIANG AND THE DRAGON'S DANCE. Illus: Ian Wallace. New York: Atheneum, 1984. Chin Chiang is afraid to do the Dragon's Dance but receives encouragement from his friend and courage from his grandfather. Age: 6-10 years.

LEGENDS

Bess, Clayton
THE TRUTH ABOUT THE MOON. Illus. Rosekrans Hoffman. Boston: Houghton Mifflin Co., 1983. A little African boy (country not indicated) wants to know why the man follows him and why the moon follows him and why the sun is hot and the moon is cold. Several explanations are provided but he is somehow not satisfied as they do not answer his questions. Age: 5-8 years.

Bruchac, Joseph & London, Jonathan
THIRTEEN MOONS ON A TURTLE'S BACK: A NATIVE AMERICAN YEAR OF MOONS. Illus: Thomas Locker. New York: Putnam and Grosset Group, 1992. Some Native American tribes believe there are thirteen moon cycles which relate to the thirteen scales on the turtle's back. This story gives one legend from each of thirteen tribes. Age: 8 years and older.

Cameron, Anne
RAVEN RETURNS THE WATER. Illus. Nelle Olsen. British Columbia, Canada: Harbour Publishing Co., Ltd. 1987. Frog drinks all the water in the world even though it is needed by other animals and plants. Frog soon learns an important lesson about sharing and so the water is restored. Age: 6-8 years.

de Paola, Tomie
THE LEGEND OF THE INDIAN PAINTBRUSH. Illus. Tomie de Paola. New York: Scholastic Inc., 1988. In this legend a little Native American boy discovers his gift is painting. He spends many days trying to get the creative spirit. Finally, to his joy and that of his People, the dream comes through. Age: 6-8 years.

Goble, Paul
IKTOMI AND THE BERRIES: A PLAINS INDIAN STORY. Illus: Paul

Goble. New York: Orchard Books, 1989. As Iktomi travels to another village he experiences many trials through his own tricks. At one time he almost falls into the water as he tries to pick some berries from the reflection in the river. Age: 5-8 years.

Goble, Paul
IKTOMI AND THE BOULDER: A PLAINS INDIAN STORY. Illus: Paul Goble. Orchard Books, New York, 1988. Iktomi is trapped by a large boulder after he takes back a blanket he gave to the boulder. Age: 5-8 years.

Goble, Paul
IKTOMI AND THE DUCKS: A PLAINS INDIAN STORY. Illus: Paul Goble. New York: Orchard Books, 1990. Iktomi got hungry while looking for his horse. He decides to trick some ducks and make a meal of them. Age: 5-8 years.

Goble, Paul
THE GIFT OF THE SACRED DOG. Illus: Paul Goble. New York: Reading Rainbow, 1980. The people were hungry and so they asked for help from the Great Spirit who sent the Sacred Dog. Age: 6-10 years.

Keens-Douglas, Richardo
FREEDOM CHILD OF THE SEA. Illus: Julia Gukova. Toronto, Canada: Annick Press, Ltd. 1995. A young boy, whose body is covered with welts and scars, lives in the sea. He is the Freedom Child of the Sea and his scarred body carries the pain his people suffered as they were transported on slave ships. Age: 8 and older.

McDermott, Gerald
ANANSI THE SPIDER: A TALE FROM THE ASHANTI. Illus. Gerald McDermott. New York: Henry Holt and Company, 1972. This is a West African legend which describes how Anansi falls into trouble and has difficulty deciding which of his sons should get the reward of the moon. Age: 3-8 years.

Mosel, Arlene (Retold by)
TIKKI TIKKI TEMBO. Illus. Blair Lent. New York: Scholastic Inc., 1968. After Chang, a Chinese boy, falls in a well and is saved, his brother falls in the well. But Chang has difficulty getting help because of an old tradition related to the first born son. Age: 6-8 years.

Osofsky, Audrey
DREAM CATCHER. Illus. Ed Young. New York: Orchard Books, 1992. An Ojibway girl makes a dream maker for her infant sibling so that the bad dreams can be taken away. Age: 7-10 years.

The Sechelt Nation
MAYUK THE GRIZZLY BEAR: LEGEND OF THE SECHELT PEOPLE. Illus. Charles Craigan. British Columbia, Canada: Nightwood Editions, 1993. Joe La Dally, an Elder of the Sechelt People surprises his People when he names his great grandson, Mayuk, the name of the grizzly bear, their foe. Age: 7-10 years.

LIFESTYLE /CUSTOM

Barth, Claire Hoffman
THE WORLD'S CHILDREN IN PICTURES: SOUTHEAST ASIA. Illus: (photographs). New York: Friendship

Press, Through the use of pictures, the life in different countries in Southeast Asia is described. Age: 7-10 years.

Chiasson, John
AFRICAN JOURNEY. Illus: John Chiasson. Bradbury Press, 1987. The lifestyle in six different communities in Africa are described. Age: 8 years and older.

Cooney, Barbara
ISLAND BOY. Illus: Barbara Cooney. Viking Penguin New York: Children's Books, 1988. This story is about the life of Matthias Tibbetts. It chronicles struggles of three generations in this rural town in Maine. Age: 3-8 years.

Musgrove, Margaret
ASHANTI TO ZULU. Illus: Leo and Diane Dillon. New York: Gryphon House, 1990. In this book the customs and lifestyles of twenty-six peoples from different African nations are described. Age: 5-8 years.

Polacco, Patricia
THE KEEPING QUILT. Illus. Patricia Polacco. New York: Simon and Schuster, Inc., 1988. To remind them of their homeland and family, a quilt is made by family members from clothing they contribute. The special quilt is passed from mother to daughter and is used during important celebrations. Age: 5-8 years.

Reich, Hanns
CHILDREN OF MANY LANDS. Illus. Hanns Reich. New York: Hills & Wang, 1958. A photographic journal in black and white of children in various parts of the world. Age: 3-8 years.

OCCUPATIONS

Blood, C & Link, M.
THE GOAT IN THE RUG. Illus: Nancy Winslow Parker. New York: Macmillan Publishing, 1976. This Navajo story is told by Geraldine, the goat, whose hair (mohair) is trimmed and used by Glenmae, a Navajo woman, to make a unique Navajo rug. Age: 5- 10 years.

Dobrin, Arnold
JOSEPHINE'S IMAGINATION: A TALE OF HAITI. Illus: Arnold Dobrin. New York: Scholastic Inc., 1973. Josephine's mother has a difficult time making money selling brooms in the market. From encouragement received from a man in the market, Josephine uses her imagination which gives her and her mother some money. Age: 6-8 years.

Hamanaka, Sheila and Ohmi, Ayano
IN SEARCH OF THE SPIRIT: THE LIVING NATIONAL TREASURES OF JAPAN. Illus: Sheila Hamanaka. New York: Morrow Junior Books, 1993. The author describes Japanese attitude toward mastery of art and the painstaking road six men take to reach and practice at mastery level. Age: 8 years and older.

Stolz, Mary
ZEKMET THE STONE CARVER: A TALE OF ANCIENT EGYPT. Illus: Deborah Nourse Lattimore. New York: Harcourt, 1988. In addition to the Pyramid, Pharaoh commands the making of a monument. This Egyptian story

describes the stone carver's attempt to construct the great Sphinx. Age: 7-9 years.

Williams, Sherley Anne
WORKING COTTON. Illus. Carole Byard. New York: Harcourt Brace and Co., 1992. A little girl describes the daily life of her family as they pick cotton for their livelihood. Age: 6-10 years.

PLANTS

Cherry, Lynne
THE GREAT KAPOK TREE. Illus: Lynne Cherry. New York: Gulliver Books, 1990. A woodsman is in the rainforest to cut down trees. While taking a short nap he is visited by several animals, and a child from the Yonomano tribe, who show the importance of the rainforest for their survival. Age: 6-8 years.

Hughes, Monica
A HANDFUL OF SEEDS. Illus. Luis Garqay. New York: Orchard Books, 1993. When Conception's grandmother dies she is forced to move to the Barrio. But she is determined to continue her grandmother's tradition which helps her and some other children to have food. Age: 5-10 years.

McCloskey, Robert
BLUEBERRIES FOR SAL. Illus: Robert McCloskey. New York: Scholastic Inc., 1948. Sal and her mother went out to collect blueberries for the winter but so do Little Bear and his mother. Sal and Little Bear are temporarily lost but are eventually united with their parents. Age: 4-8 years.

Williams, Vera B.
CHERRIES AND CHERRY PITS. Illus: Vera B. Williams. New York: Scholastic inc., 1986. Bidemmi's friend likes to visit her as she draws and tell stories about cherries and cherry pits. Age: 4-8 years.

RACE RELATIONS

Coleman, Evelyn
WHITE SOCKS ONLY. Illus: Tyrone Geter. Chicago, Ill.: Albert Whitman and Co., Morton Greene, 1996. An African-American grandmother tells how as a little girl she went into town and drank from the "Whites Only" fountain because she was wearing white socks. This results in some unexpected changes. Age: 5 years and older.

Coles, Robert
THE STORY OF RUBY BRIDGES. Illus: George Ford. New York: Scholastic, Inc., 1995. A young African-American girl is chosen to integrate one of the public schools in Louisiana. This story describes what transpires as parents fight to keep the school segregated. Age: 6 and older.

Greene, Carla
MANUEL, YOUNG MEXICAN AMERICAN. Illus: Haris Petie. New York: Lantern Press, Inc., 1969. A little Mexican boy has difficulty making friends and becoming a member of the neighborhood baseball team simply because he is Mexican. Age: 7 and older.

Mochizuki, Ken
BASEBALL SAVED US. Illus: Don Lee. New York: Lee and Low Books, 1993. A

Japanese boy learns to play baseball while in a Japanese Internment Camp in the United States during WWII. When his family gets out he faces prejudice and discrimination because he is Japanese. Age: 6-10 years.

Sebestyen, Ouida
WORDS BY HEART. New York: Bantam Books, 1979. Lena wanted to show she had a Magic mind so people would focus on her ability rather than the color of her skin. However, winning the memory content was a far less challenge than trying to keep the promise she made to her father as he lay dying. Age: 9 years and older.

Shange, Ntozake
WHITE WASH. Illus: Michael Sporn. New York: Walker and Co., 1997. Helene-Angel, a young African-American is spray painted white by a gang of white boys as she and her brother travel home from school. This leaves her traumatized. Soon her friends come to her support. Age: 6-10 years.

Taylor, Mildred
THE FRIENDSHIP. Illus: Max Ginsburg. New York: Bantam Books, 1987. After Mr. Tom Bee, an African-American, saves John Wallace's life, John promises him they would be friends forever. However, the friendship is tested and something terrible results. Age: 8 years and older.

Taylor, Mildred
THE GOLD CADILLAC. Illus: Michael Hays. New York: Bantam Books, 1987. When 'lois's and Wilma's father traded in the Mercury that was less than a year old for a brand new 1950 Coupe de Ville, their mother was furious. However, nothing could prepare them for the humiliation they would suffer later when they take a long trip.
Age: 8 years and older.

Vigna, Judith
BLACK LIKE KYRA, WHITE LIKE ME. Illus: Judith Vigna. Morton Grove, Ill: Albert Whitman and Co., 1992. Christy is overjoyed that her friend Kyra and her family are moving next door. However, some white neighbors treat them badly. Soon the family that treats them the worst moves away. Age: 5-10 years.

Woodson, Jacqueline
THE OTHER SIDE. Illus: E. B. Lewis. G. P. New York: Putnam's Sons, 2001. Clover is African American and Annie is White. They each live on a different side of the fence. Both are told not to go over the fence so eventually they both end up sitting on the fence together. Age: 5 and older.

RHYMES AND POEMS

Brooks, Gwendolyn
ALONENESS. Illus: Leroy Foster. Detroit, MI: Broadside Press, 1971. A child explains the difference between loneliness and aloneness and why aloneness is so much better than loneliness. Age: 6-8 years.

Clifton, Lucille
SOME OF THE DAYS OF EVERETT ANDERSON. Illus. New York: Holt, Rinehart & Winston, 1970. Everett

Anderson, once again, faces some childhood issues. These are described in the book. Age: 6-8 years.

Dragonwagon, Crescent
HALF A MOON AND ONE WHOLE STAR. Illus: Jerry Pinkney. New York: Aladdin Books, 1990. Using poetry, the story tells what happens at night with the animals, the flowers and Johnny, the saxophonist, while Susan, an African American girl and her family sleep. Age: 4-6 years.

Giovanni, Nikki
SPIN A SOFT BLACK SONG. Illus. George Martins. New York: Farrar Straus and Giroux, 1991. Giovanni weaves her magic as these poems, many of which are written in dialect, are spoken in the voice of African-American children. Age: 6-8 years.

Greenfield, Eloise
HONEY I LOVE AND OTHER LOVE POEMS. Illus. Diane and Leon Dillon. New York: Harper Trophy, 1986. Fifteen wonderful poems written in vivid language about aspects of African-American life. Age: 4-10 years.

Greenfield, Eloise
UNDER THE SUNDAY TREE. Illus: (paintings) Amos Ferguson. New York: Harper & Row, 1988. Twenty poems about life in the Bahamas. Through the poems and the paintings the reader/listener becomes acquainted with the culture of country. Age: 5-10 years.

Joseph, Lynn
COCONUT KIND OF DAY: ISLAND POEMS. Illus. Sandra Speidel. New York: Puffin Books, 1990. Using the language and tone of the Caribbean, this book of poems describes life in Trinidad. Age: 6-10 years.

Kroll, Virginia
JAHA AND JAMIL WENT DOWN THE HILL: AN AFRICAN MOTHER GOOSE. Illus. Katherine Roundtree. MA: Charlesbridge Publishing, 1995. A book of Mother Goose rhymes depicting life in Africa. Some rhymes are recognizable. However, the lyrics are different and quite interesting. Age: 5-8 years.

Lillegard, Dee
MY FIRST MARTIN LUTHER KING BOOK. Illus: Dee Lillegard. New York: Gryphon House, 1990. This book of poetry, for young readers, depicts the life of Martin Luther King, Jr., an African-American. Age: 4-8 years.

Little, Lessie Jones
CHILDREN OF LONG AGO. Illus: Jan Spivey Gilchrist. New York: Philomel Books, 1988. Through verses, the poet describes, what her own life was like in a black farming community in the Rural South. Age: 6 years and older.

Siebert, Diane
MOJAVE. Illus: Wendell Minor. Crowell, 1988. Through the voice of Mojave these poems describe life in the Mojave desert. Age: 6-10 years.

SEASONS

Clifton, Lucille
THE BOY WHO DIDN'T BELIEVE IN SPRING. Illus. Turkle Brinton. New

York: E. P. Dutton, 1973. King Shabazz and his friend Anthony Polita did not believe in spring until they had an interesting discovery. Age: 5-8 years.

SELF-AWARENESS/SELF-ESTEEM

Anno, Mitsumasa
THE KING'S FLOWER. Illus: Anno Mitsumasa.. New York: Collins,1979. The King wanted everything he had extra large but when he planted a tulip to make it the largest flower in the world, it only grew to regular size. Age: 4-8 years.

Ashley, Bernard
CLEVERSTICKS. Illus: Derk Brazell. New York: Crown Publishers, 1991. Ling Sing didn't like school because he couldn't do anything the other children could do. Then he discovered he could use chopsticks and the other children and teachers could not. Age: 4-8 years.

Blue, R.
I AM HERE/ YO ESTOY AQUI. Illus. R. Blue. Oxford: Franklin Watts, 1971. The story describes some of the difficulties of a little Puerto Rican child who begins kindergarten with Spanish as his language tool. Age 5-9 years.

Cannon, Janell
STELLALUNA. Illus: Janell Cannon.. New York: Harcourt Brace and Co., 1993. A bat is separated from her mother. She falls into a bird's nest and thinks she is a bird until she comes in contact with some bats and they set her straight. Age: 4-8 years.

Carle, Eric
THE MIXED-UP CHAMELEON. Illus: Eric Carle. New York: Harper Trophy,1984.The chameleon was not happy with who he was and kept wishing to be someone else. When he had difficulty catching a fly, he wished to be himself again. Age: 5-8 years.

Caudhill, Rebecca
DID YOU CARRY THE FLAG TODAY, CHARLIE? Illus. Nancy Grossman. New York: Dell Publishing, 1966. The highest honor in a little Appalachian school is to have the child who is most helpful carry the flag that day. It was quite a surprise when Charley was chosen. Age: 5-8 years.

Clifton, Lucille
ALL US COME CROSS THE WATER. Illus: John Steptoe. New York: Holt, Rinehart & Winston, 1973. The story describes Ujamaa's frustration because his teacher doesn't recognize his identity as being from a particular country in Africa as opposed to Africa, the continent. Age: 7-9 years.

Cohen, Barbara
MOLLY'S PILGRIM. Illus: Daniel Mark Duffy. New York: Lothrop, Lee & Shepard, 1993. Molly moved to the United States from Russia. She is not having a good time at school until Thanksgiving when she realizes that not everyone is the same. Age: 6 and older.

Cuyler, Margery
FROM HERE TO THERE. Illus: Yu Cha Pak. New York: Henry Holt and Co., 1999. A little girl discovers her place in the universe as she looks at herself in

different situations and circumstances. Age: 5-10 years.

Freeman, Don
DANDELION. Illus: Don Freeman. New York: Viking Press, 1964. Jennifer Giraffe invited lion to her party but he almost missed the party because of his vanity. Age: 4-7 years.

Guarino, Deborah
IS YOUR MAMA A LLAMA? Illus: Steven Kellog. New York: Scholastic, Inc., 1989. Told in rhyme, this story is about a llama who does not know what it's mama looks like so the llama asks all the animals if their mama is a llama. Age: 3- 6 years.

Hamanaka, Sheila.
ALL THE COLORS OF THE EARTH. Illus: Sheila Hamanaka.. New York: Morrow Junior Books, 1994. Various colors of the earth are described. These colors are then matched to the variety of skin and hair color as well as hair type of children. Age: 4-10 years.

Heide, Florence P. & Gillian, Judith Heide
THE DAYS OF AHMED'S SECRET. Illus: Ted Lewin. New York: Mulberry Press, 1990. Ahmed, a little Egyptian boy has a secret which he carries with him as he works for his father delivering bottles. At the end of the day he reveals his secret. Age:5-8 years.

Herron, Carolivia
NAPPY HAIR. Illus: Joe Cepeda. New York: Alfred Knopf, 1997. Brenda's nappy hair is celebrated in Uncle Mordecai's call-response story told at the family's backyard picnic. Age: 5-10 years.

Hoffman, Mary
AMAZING GRACE. Illus. Caroline Binch. New York: Dial Books, 1990. Grace believes she can do anything. However, she is met with opposition when she wants to play the part of Peter Pan. With support and encouragement from her mother and grandmother she achieves her goal. Age:5-10 years.

Hoffman, Mary
NANCY NO SIZE. Illus: Jennifer Northway. Oxford: Franklin Watts, 1987. Nancy is the middle member in her biracial family. She never seems to fit in always being too short or too small. One day, however, Nancy is able to take a special place and become very happy as a result. Age: 3-8 years.

Hudson, Cheryl & Ford, Bernette
BRIGHT EYES, BROWN SKIN. Illus. George Ford. Orange, New Jersey: Just Us Books, 1990. Four bright-eyed African-American children are engaged in activities that children normally do. The rhyming and the detailed illustrations provide a positive image and delightful reading. Age: 3-6 years

Katz, Karen
THE COLOR OF US. Illus: Karen Katz. New York: Henry Holt and Co., 1999. Lena, a little Hispanic girl, wants to paint a picture of herself so her mother, who is an artist, takes her out to see the variation of people's skin color which is compared to different foods. Age: 5:8 years.

Keats, Ezra Jack
WHISTLE FOR WILLIE. Illus: Ezra jack Keats. New York: Puffin Books, 1977. Peter, a little Hispanic boy, wants to be able to whistle to call his dog. He keep practicing until finally one day he discovers he is able to whistle. He then started whistling all the time. Age: 3-8 years.

Kline, Suzy
SONG LEE IN ROOM 2B. Illus: Frank Remkiewicz. New York: Scholastic, Inc., 1993. A little Korean girl is nervous about giving a presentation about her country. Accompanied by her mother and dressed as a tree she does a great job holding the attention of even the problem student. Age: 6-10 years.

Lowlier, Laurie
HOW TO SURVIVE THE THIRD GRADE. Illus: Joyce Addy Czarinas. New York: Whitman Publishing, 1988. Ernest is an outcast because he is small. Mugwana, a new arrival from Kenya, helps Ernest to overcome many things. Age: 7-9 years.

Lionni, Leo
A COLOR OF HIS OWN. Illus. Leo Lionni. New York: Alfred Knopf, 1975. The chameleon wants to have a color of his own but learns from another chameleon that is not possible. They then travel together and change colors together. Age: 3-8 years.

Little, Leslie Jones & Greenfield, Eloise
I CAN DO IT BY MYSELF. Illus: Carol Byard. New York: Gryphon House, 1990. A little African American boy reaches a point when he wants to establish his

independence. He keeps trying to do everything himself. Age: 4-7 Years.

Nikola, Lisa
BEIN' WITH YOU THIS WAY. Illus: Michael Bryant. New York: Lee and Bow Books, Inc., 1994. This story depicts a variety of children and adults in ways which show how much we are alike but different. Each page, asks for audience response as it repeats then adds a new descriptions. Age: 3-8 years.

Say, Allen
EMMA'S RUG. Illus: Allen Say. New York: Houghton Mifflin Co., 1996A young Japanese artist discovers that her creativity really comes from within when a rug, on which she usually relies for inspiration, is destroyed. Age: 6 years and older.

Say, Allen
STRANGER IN THE MIRROR. New York: Houghton Mifflin Co., 1995. A young Japanese boy wakes up with the face of an old man and people begin to see him differently. Age: 3-10 years.

Simon, Norma
WHY AM I DIFFERENT? Illus: Dora Leder. New York: Gryphon House, 1990. Children first notice differences. This book explains differences and attempts to help children understand differences in a positive way. Age: 4-8 years.

Tabor, Nancy Maria Grande.
WE ARE A RAINBOW. Illus: Nancy Maria Grande Tabor. Watertown, MA: Charlesbridge Publishing, 1997. The author describes how although people may have come from different cultures

there can still be many similarities as well as differences. Age: 3-8 years.

Yarbrough, Camille
CORNROWS. Illus: Carole Byard. New York: The Putnam and Grosset Group, 1979. The braided hairstyle, cornrows, originated in ancient Africa where the style of the cornrow was used to identify clans, villages and religions. Today the styles are named after outstanding African Americans to depict their courage. Ages: 4-10 years.

SELF-DISCOVERY

Blackman, Malorie
A NEW DRESS FOR MAYA. Illus: Rhian Nest James. Milwaukee: Gareth Stevens Children's Books, 1991. Maya, a little African American girl, is sad and upset. She is going to Anna's party and wants to wear a new dress. However, in the end, she decides to wear the dress her mother made. Age: 3-8 years.

Paek, Min
AEKYUNG'S DREAM. Illus: Min Paek. New York: Children's Press, 1988. Aekyung is Korean. The children tease her and call her "Chinese Eyes" and she does not correct them. Then her tells her about her culture and she becomes proud enough to admit she is Korean. Age: 6 and older.

Snyder, Diane
THE BOY OF THE THREE-YEAR NAP. Illus: Allen Say. New York: Houghton Mifflin Co., 1988. A Japanese woman's lazy son wants to marry a rich man's daughter. His mother twisted the plan so the son ends up working for the rich man. Age: 6-10.

Waters, Kate & Slovenz-Low, Madeline
LION DANCER: ERNIE WAN'S CHINESE NEW YEAR. Photographs by Martha Cooper. New York: Scholastic, Inc., 1990. It is an important day for Ernie Wan. He is to perform the Lion Dance in the parade in the streets of New York. Age: 7-10 years.

Wells, Rosemary
YOKO. Illus: Rosemary Wells. New York: Hypernion Books, 1998. The children are unfamiliar with sushi so they make fun of Yoko, a young Japanese girl who takes sushi to school for lunch then one student tries it and things change for Yoko. Age: 5-10 years.

Wyeth, Sharon Dennis
SOMETHING BEAUTIFUL. Illus; Chris K. Soentpiet. New York: Dragonfly Books, 1998. A young African-American girl, who lives in the inner city, searches for something beautiful. Age: 5-8 years.

SEPARATION AND LOSS

Boholm-Olsson, Eva
TUAN. Translated by Diane Jonasson, illustrated by Pham Van Don. R & S/Farrar, 1988. The story describes Tuan, a Vietnamese boy, who now lives with only his mother because his father died. Tuan has difficulty dealing with the situation.
Age: 5-8 years.

Clifton, Lucille
EVERETT ANDERSON'S GOODBYE.
Illus: Ann Grifalconi. New York:
Gryphon House, 1990. This story is about
Everett Anderson, a little African-
American boy, who upon the death of his
father goes through the stages of grief.
Age: 4-8 years.

TIME CONCEPT

Anno, Mitsumasa
ALL IN A DAY. Illus. Anno Mitsumasa.
New York: Philomel Books, N.Y. 1986.
Through the use of illustrations depicting
different countries, authors from different
countries compile a comparison of what
people would be doing in different parts
of the world starting from 6:00 p.m.
December 31 to 9:00 a.m. January 2. The
drawings and explanations show the
similarities and differences among people
in different parts of the world. Age: 6
years and older.

Kandoian, Ellen
IS ANYBODY UP? Illus: Ellen
Kandoian. New York: Putnam, 1989.
Describes what people are doing at the
same time in different parts of the world.
Age: 3-8 years.

WEATHER

Anderson, Lonzo.
THE DAY THE HURRICANE
HAPPENED. Illus: Ann Grifalconi. New
York: Charles Scribner's Sons, 1974. A
family struggles to protect themselves,
their crop and their animals against a
hurricane that hits the island of St. Johns
in the Virgin Islands. Ages: 6-10 years.

Hamilton, Virginia
DRYLONGSO. Illus: Jerry Pinkney. New
York: Harcourt Brace and Company,
1992. Drylongso is blown into town by a
wall of dust created by drought. He is
welcomed into a family and helps them
irrigate the land. Age 7-10 years.

Keats, Ezra Jack
THE SNOWY DAY. Illus. Ezra Jack
Keats. New York: Viking Press, Peter, a
little Hispanic boy, decided to go out in
the snow one snowy day. His activities
include the building of a snowman,
making a snow angel and taking home
snow in his pocket. Age: 3-8 years.

Yashima, Taro
UMBRELLA. Illus: Taro Yashima. The
New York: Viking Press, 1958. A little
Japanese girl gets red rubber boots and an
umbrella for her third birthday and her
mother will not let her wear the boots or
use the umbrella until it rains. Age: 3-6
years.

Author's Notes On Integrated Curriculum

In today's classroom, it is imperative that the teacher takes into consideration not only the developmental levels of children but also the diverse backgrounds from which students come. For the curriculum to be effective, it must build upon prior knowledge (Piaget & Inhelder, 1969). However, as John Dewey espoused during the progressive movement, the curriculum also needs to be integrated so children can make connections to the various content areas (Dworkin, 1959).

Difference Between Themes and Units

According to Roopnarine and Johnson (1993), there is a difference between themes and units. Themes tend to have broad vague titles that do not indicate the direction the work will take. Themes also typically do not provide an indication of what children will know at the end of the theme cycle. However, units typically consist of a sequence of prespecified lessons on particular topics. A unit, therefore, is an example of an integrated approach to teaching. The goals and, ultimately, the experiences, are arranged around a particular theme. Activities should be multidisciplinary. This allows the children to see the connections across curriculum areas.

Multicultural Books and the Integrated Curriculum

The integrated curriculum is based on the belief that young children learn holistically. Information, therefore, should be provided as a whole and not as bits and pieces of information. A well planned curriculum is a very important part of any early childhood program. Therefore, a literature-based integrated curriculum is ideal for supporting content areas (Jalongo, 1992; Morrow, 1997; Wortham, 1998; Seefeldt, 2001). This is applicable whether the teacher is using a unit- or theme-based curriculum approach. Multicultural literature, like mainstream literature is ideal for supporting such a curriculum.

Although, understandably, some topics are curriculum-driven, it is important to allow the children to make some decisions regarding the topic since they will choose topics that are of interest to them. However, once the topic is chosen the onus is on the teacher to decide on the goals and objectives for the theme or unit and the concepts, skills and values to be taught in the lesson.

Content Areas:

There is a tendency to focus multicultural education on areas such as language arts and social studies. However, multicultural literature can be used in any area of the curriculum. Also, although content areas tend to be taught separately an integrated curriculum approach shows how content areas are interconnected. For example, some books that can support science such as *A Handful of Seeds* (Hughes, 1993), and *Seedfolks* (Fleishman, 1997), can also be used for a lesson in social studies, art and mathematics *The Snowy Day* (Keats, 1975), can be used to support a unit or theme about weather. Once again, this story can also support social studies, art and mathematics.

Another story, *Follow the Drinking Gourd* (Winter, 1988), has a more historical perspective. It demonstrates the need to understand the position of the stars (science). Without this knowledge, the slaves would probably not have been able to make their escape in the Underground Railroad. *Rehema's Journey* (Margolies, 1990), is another story that can be used for science. The story describes the growing and preparation of the foods eaten and some of the physical aspects of the environment. Aspects in both stories are also applicable to social studies, art and math.

Other books which could support a science unit include *Anancy and the Hide-Away Garden, In Spiderman Anancy* (Berry, 1988). This story describe the luscious fruits and vegetables in the garden Anansi discovered. *The Great Kapok Tree* (Cherry, 1990), alerts the reader to how people and animals benefit from the rainforests. In this story the animals and a little boy from the Yanomano tribe approach the woodcutter to explain how they need the rainforest. This story also supports a study of the rainforest and its importance to the environment, especially in protecting the ozone layer.

A unit on food can be dealt with from a science, social studies, math or language arts perspective using books such as: *Strawberry Thanksgiving* (Jennings, 1992), and *Cherries and Cherry Pits* (Williams, 1986).

Another story, *The Tortilla Factory* (Paulsen, 1995), describes planting the corn to how tortillas are made. Children for whom the tortilla is a staple, would delight in the inclusion of this story. Making tortillas would include content areas such as science, mathematics, social studies, language arts as well as art. This type of integration approach would help children learn about tortillas in a more holistic and authentic way.

Blueberries for Sal (McCloskey, 1976) and *Too Many Tamales* (Soto & Martinez, 1993), are some other books that could also easily support a unit on food. The teacher can bring in blueberries for counting and tasting and also a recipe for blueberry muffins. Some children may not be familiar with tamales and so a cooking activity would prove very useful. However, teachers need to be cognizant of the fact that not all children are familiar with all foods, not even all the foods in the United States. Also, children from different regions may know a different name for the same food. This may be especially true for children from a different culture. The sweet potato (called yams), for example, is a totally different vegetable in some tropical countries. Also, the eggplant is known as "garden egg" in some cultures.

Although teachers may prefer to use specific books to support certain topics, almost any book could support a content area. *Dumpling Soup* (Rattigan, 1993), describes not only the relationship in a multicultural family but also how New Year's Eve is celebrated in Hawaii. Much information is provided about the members of the family and how the soup is made. Such a book could easily support a unit as it contains material for math, science, social studies, language arts and art. For older children history and geography can also be added separately.

Although the socio-cultural aspect is the focus in the *It Takes a Village* (Cowen-Fletcher, 1994), a scientific aspect can also be applied as children learn about local markets and the foods they sell. Children can also learn why some foods are sold day-to-day, how the supermarkets keep foods fresh, and how to check foods for spoilage. A follow-up activity could include a trip to the market to price and purchase items for a recipe for cooking. This facilitates the content areas of social studies, mathematics, language arts and science. Although language arts and social studies can be further integrated by discussing food production, supply and demand and have children research and write about their findings, this need not be the focus.

Teachers need to plan the curriculum so that children, even in a homogeneous classroom, gain a broad perspective of the world. Teachers also need to ensure that all groups are represented in a fair and unbiased way (Wortham, 1998; Klein, 1995; Banks, 1999; Marshall, 2001; Gollnick & Chinn 2002). Multicultural books with their diversity of content, can support the curriculum in numerous and exciting ways. Their effectiveness, however, is left to the creativity and imagination of the teacher.

Appendix A

An Example of Some Additional Multicultural Books That Support An Integrated Curriculum

Language Arts:

Berry, J. (1988). Anancy and the Hide-Away Garden. In *Spiderman Anancy*,

Carle, E. (1987). The Very Hungry Caterpillar.

Clifton, L. (1973). The Boy Who Didn't Believe In Spring.

Feelings, M. (1974). Jambo Means Hello: Swahili Alphabet Book.

Grifalconi, A. (1986). The Village of Round and Square Houses.

Williams, S.A. (1975). Working Cotton.

Science:

Cherry, L. (1990). The Great Kapok Tree: A Tale of the Amazon Rain Forest.

Hughes, M. (1993). A Handful of Seeds

Margolies, B. (1990). Rehema's Journey: A Visit to Tanzania

McCloskey, R. (1976). Blueberries for Sal.

Nikly, M. (1982). The Emperor's Plum Tree

Williams, V. (1986). Cherries and Cherry Pits

Mathematics:

Blood, C. & Link, M. (1976). The Goat in the Rug.

Feelings, M. (1971). Moja Means One: A Swahili Counting Book.

Kimmel, E. A. (1988). Anansi and the Moss-Covered Rock

Porter, A. (1991). Kwanzaa

Social Studies:

Aardema, V. (1981). Bringing the Rain to Kapiti Plain.

Bang, M. (1985). The Paper Crane

Goble, P. (1989). Iktomi and the Berries.

Jennings, P. (1992). Strawberry Thanksgiving.

Rylant, C. (1985). The Relatives Came.

Rylant, C. (1982). When I Was Young In the Mountains.

Soto, G. & Martinez, E. (1993). Too Many Tamales.

Art:

Beskow, E. (1971). Pelle's New Suit.

dePaola, T. (1973). Charlie Needs A Cloak

dePaola, T. (1988). The Legend of the Indian Paintbrush

Some Children's Books in Spanish

Aruego, Jose & Ariane (1972). *Cuento de un Cocodrilo: Historia Popular Filipina.* Scholastic Inc., N. Y.

Behrens, June (1985). *Fiesta: Cinco de Mayo.* Children's Press, Chicago.

Bornstein, Ruth (1976). *Gorilita.* Scholastic Inc., N. Y.

Johnson, T & dePaola, T. (1985). *La Historia de una Colcha.* Scholastic Inc., N. Y.

Mahy, M. (1990). *Los Siete Hermanos Chinos.* Scholastic Inc., N. Y.

Matthias, C. (1988). *Los Gatos Me Gustan Mas.* Children's Press, N. Y.

McKissack, P. & McKissack, F. (1989). *El Traje Nuevo Del Emperador.* Children's Press, Chicago.

Munsch, R. (1983). *El Papa de David.* Editorial Annick Press Ltd., Toronto, Canada.

Numeroff, L. (1991). *Si Le Das Un Panecillo A Un Alce.* Scholastic Inc., N. Y.

Rowe, E. (1973). *Los Dinosaurios Gigantes.* Scholastic Inc., N. Y.

Slobodkina, E. Se Venden Gorras: *La Historia de un Vendedor Ambulannte, Unos Monos y Sus Travesuras.* Scholastic inc., N. Y.

Soto, G. *El Maullido de la Gata.* Scholastic Inc., N. Y.

Appendix B

**Some Activities that Can Be Used To Support
Multicultural Book Content**

Language Arts

Activity:	*Something's Fishy – Fish Contraction*
Skill:	Matching Contraction to word that forms contraction
Age/Grade Level:	8-10 Years
Book that can be used with this project:	McKissack, P. (1992). *A Million Fish .... More or Less*. Illus: Dena Schutzer. New York: Alfred Knopf Publishing.
	All the contractions in this activity are from the story listed above. Using the fish cutouts, match the contractions to the words to which they belong.
Materials:	Scissors Markers 18 cut outs of fish

Procedure:

1. On one half of fish write contraction and on the other half write the two words that make up the contraction.
2. Laminate
3. Cut out each fish and then cut in half (in a variety of zig-zag fashions)
4. Have children match the two halves
5. Provide Answer Key for children who may need it.

Something's Fishy – Fish Contraction

Clues:

1.	'T was	10.	That's
2.	Didn't	11.	It'll
3.	I'm	12.	I'll
4.	Let's	13.	Wouldn't
5.	Wasn't	14.	It's
6.	What's	15.	Can't
7.	I've	16.	You've
8.	We'll	17.	Don't
9.	What 'll	18.	Hadn't

Turn to the next page for answers.

Answers:

	Contractions	Words for Contractions
1.	'Twas	It was
2.	Didn't	Did not
3.	I'm	I am
4.	Let's	Let us
5.	Wasn't	Was not
6.	What's	What is
7.	I've	I have
8.	We'll	We will
9.	What' ll	What will
10.	That's	That is
11.	It'll	It will
12.	I'll	I will
13.	Wouldn't	Would not
14.	It's	It is
15.	Can't	Can not
16.	You've	You have
17.	Don't	Do not
18.	Hadn't	Had not

Suggestion to Broaden Cultural Awareness:

Fishing is a common activity in many cultures. It can be a source of income or a source of pleasure. Although many children will be familiar with the concept of fishing, some children may not. Introduce the fishing game (using cut out of fish, yarn and magnet).

Have the children research and discuss different types of fish and where they are most likely to be located. For example saltwater and freshwater.

Activity:	*Comprehension Wheel*
	Match the answer on clothes pin to the question on the wheel.
Skill:	Recalling facts Matching
Age/Grade Level:	7-10 Years
Book that can be used with this project:	Say, A. (1982). *The Bicycle Man.* Illus: Allen Say. Boston: Houghton Mifflin Co.
Materials:	Question Wheel Poster board Large clothes pins Scissors Pen/Marker

Procedure:

1. Glue the Question Wheel to poster board and laminate
2. Write each of the answers (from the following page) on a clothespin
3. Have the students match the answer on each clothespin to the question

Check answers on page 60.

Check answers on page 60.

Comprehension Wheel

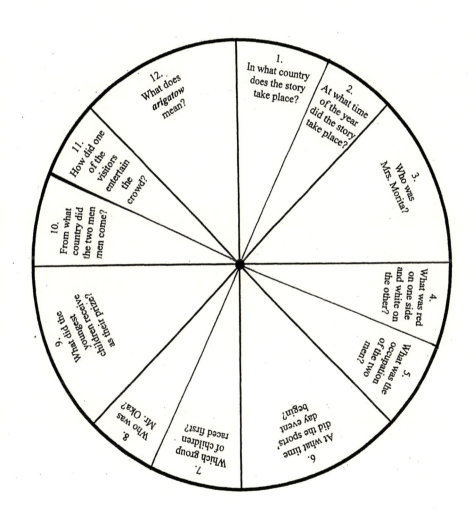

1. In what country does the story take place?

2. At what time of the year did the story take place?

3. Who was Mrs. Morita?

4. What was red on one side and white on the other?

5. What was the occupation of the two men?

6. At what time did the sports' day event begin?

7. Which group of children raced first?

8. Who was Mr. Oka?

9. What did the youngest children receive as their prize?

10. From what country did the two men come?

11. How did one of the visitors entertain the crowd?

12. What does *arigatow* mean?

Answer Key:

Questions		Answers	
1.	In what country does the story take place?	1.	South Island of Japan
2.	At what time of the year did the story take place?	2.	Spring
3.	Who was Mrs. Morita?	3.	First grade teacher
4.	What was red on one side and white on the other?	4.	The head bands
5.	What was the occupation of the two men?	5.	They were soldiers
6.	At what time did the sports' day event begin?	6.	Nine o'clock
7.	Which group of children raced first?	7.	The youngest group
8.	Who was Mr. Oka?	8.	He is the art teacher
9.	What did the youngest children receive as their prize?	9.	Oranges, rice cakes and pencils
10.	From what country did the two men come?	10.	They were from the United States.
11.	How did one of the visitors entertain the crowd?	11.	He rode and did tricks on the principal's bicycle
12.	What does ***arigatow*** mean?	12.	It means "Thank You."

Comprehension Wheel.

Suggestion to Broaden Cultural Awareness:

Sporting events are an important part of many cultures. Children across many cultures are familiar with the concept of "Sports Day." Find out about different types of sports across different cultures, for example, cricket, soccer, etc. Also, have children research types of games children play during sports day, e.g. Egg and Spoon race, Sack Race Tug and War, Chinese Jump Rope, etc.

Have the children participate in "Sack Race" or a sport from another culture. (Children step into a sack and jump toward the finish line. First one to reach is the winner). Ask the children to compare their sports day to the one described in the story. They can also be asked to research types of sports events in other cultures.

This is also a good opportunity to discuss transportation. There are various forms of transportation used in different cultures. Children may be familiar with transportation as they relate to land, air and sea. However, aside from the economic aspect, land form and weather may impact the mode of transportation used. Why, for example, is the bicycle a popular mode of transportation in Japan and the gondola in Venice, Italy?. Have the children research the mode of transportation used in other cultures (land, air and sea), and the reasons for the types of transportation, for example, camel, horse, cars, boats such as the gondola, rickshaw, dray, etc.).

62

Activity:	*Comparing Two Stories*
Skill:	Compare and Contrast Recognizing Similarities and Differences Using a Venn Diagram
Age/Grade:	6-10 Years
Books that can be used with this project:	Slobodkina, E. (1968). *Caps for Sale: A Tale of A Peddler, Some Monkeys and their Business.* Illus: Esphyr Slobodkina. New York: Harper Trophy.
	Diakite, B. W. (1999). *The Hatseller and the Monkeys: A West African Folktale.* Illus: Baba Wague Diakite. New York: Scholastic, Inc.

There are many similarities and differences in the stories listed below. In each side of the Venn diagram show how the stories are different and in the middle of the Venn diagram show how both stories are alike.

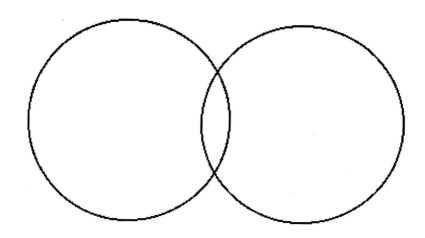

Caps for Sale   Both Stories   The Hatseller and the Monkeys

Suggestion to Broaden Cultural Awareness:

Getting wares to the market sometimes involves traveling for miles. In this story one vender endures, by sheer accident, while the other by his wit. Many children will be familiar with the concept of going to the market, even if it is the supermarket.

To assist children not familiar with the open market concept, the teacher take the children on a field trip to a flea market where wares are taken in and sold openly. After the trip, discuss the experience with the children what they saw. Use an experience chart so the children can provide the information in their own words.

For older students, have them write their story and put the stories together in a book. Put the book in the classroom library.

All answers should be accepted.

Refer Word Search - *Abuela's Weave*

Note: *Countries such as Italy have this type of open market. Collect pictures and share them with the children*.

Activity: *Comparing Cinderella Stories*

Skill: Comparing story elements
                             Recognizing similarities and differences

Age/grade Level: 6-10 years.

Many stories have things in common. For example, all stories have certain characteristics. The Cinderella stories have much more in common. They depict good overcoming evil. The chart on the following page shows how the Cinderella stories are alike or different in the areas listed.

Books that support
this project: Climo, S. (1993). *The Korean Cinderella*. Illus: Ruth
                             Heller. New York: Harper Collins Publishers.

                             Louie, Ai-Ling (1982). *Yeh-Shen: A Cinderella Story
                             From China*. Illus: Ed Young. New York: Philomel
                             Books.

                             Martin, R. *The Rough-Face Girl: Algonquin Indian
                             Cinderella Story*. Illus: David Shannon. New York:
                             Scholastic, Inc.

                             Perrault, C. (Trans. by Marcia Brown, 1954).
                             Cinderella Or The Little Glass Slipper. Illus: Marcia
                             Brown. New York: Charles Scribner's Sons.

                             Steptoe, J. (1990). *Mufaro's Beautiful Daughters*. Illus:
                             John Steptoe. New York: Gryphon House.

Compare the Following Cinderella Stories

Story Elements	Cinderella (traditional English version)	Yeh-Shen: Cinderella Story from China	Korean Cinderella	Mufaro's Beautiful Daughters	The Rough-Faced Girl
Setting (location, weather, time period, etc.)					
Characters (people or personified animals)					
Theme					
Style					
Plot (sequence of events/ characters in conflict/ problem)					

Suggestion to Broaden Cultural Awareness:

These Cinderella stories show how people, regardless of culture or ethnicity, draw upon their problem solving skills in their need survive or make it through a difficult situation. They also show that hard work can be rewarding.
Each story takes place in a different culture. However, in all the story situations help is provided. In each case the main character is in need of assistance and they are helped by others who are in a better situation. This shows that many of these cultures are cooperative or "helping cultures." students, therefore, can learn about the importance of cooperation.

Ask the children if they have ever been in a situation of dire need. Were they helped? By whom?

Provide the children with crayons, markers, glue, scissors, paper bags, paper plates, construction paper and newsprint. Then have them choose their favorite character from one of the stories and using the paper plate and other materials, make a puppet of that character. Older children can also write about their favorite character.

Note: Provide close supervision to younger children.

Activity: *Word Search*

Skill: Figure Ground (locating words)
                              Finding words that are the same

Age/Grade Level: 7-10 Years

Book that can be used
with this project: Pak, S. (1999). *Dear Juno*. Susan Hartung. New York:
                              Puffin Books.

In the grid on the following page are the words listed below along with some random letters. All the words are from the story. Circle all the words you can find in the grid?

When you are through, check your answer on the completed grid.

WORD LIST FROM DEAR JUNO

1.	WATCHED	11.	TEACHER
2.	BLINKING LIGHTS	12.	SWINGING
3.	SOARED	13.	BACKYARD
4.	FARAWAY	14.	BIGGEST
5.	PERSIMMONS	15.	LEAF
6.	GRANDMOTHER	16.	ENVELOPE
7.	WAGGED	17.	UNDERNEATH
8.	PHOTOGRAPH	18.	DREW
9.	CAT	19.	CRISP
10.	YELLOW	20.	UNFOLDED

Title: *Dear Juno*

W	P	K	B	Z	Q	Z	C	K	G	U	K	U	Q	S	F	M	C	Q	X
P	A	E	P	U	X	M	R	G	J	R	N	X	B	Y	O	Q	S	G	X
H	G	T	R	N	H	L	I	F	V	M	A	D	N	T	M	A	A	S	E
O	T	W	C	S	M	W	S	D	D	F	S	N	E	P	K	R	R	P	Z
T	D	I	P	H	I	X	P	B	W	W	W	B	D	R	D	U	M	E	A
O	U	R	O	X	E	M	H	V	A	H	I	A	N	M	N	J	Z	O	D
G	N	W	E	H	Y	D	M	W	C	Y	N	C	D	S	O	E	C	E	I
R	F	P	B	W	E	H	F	O	D	T	G	K	C	I	T	T	A	B	N
A	O	F	S	P	L	J	Y	E	N	O	I	Y	G	U	N	Q	H	T	W
P	L	T	S	L	L	E	L	S	Z	S	N	A	D	E	E	Y	X	E	H
H	D	N	N	W	O	K	N	O	H	R	G	R	U	W	D	R	M	J	R
V	E	P	M	T	W	A	N	V	G	L	Y	D	N	V	S	E	Y	Z	P
C	D	H	Y	R	L	R	U	P	E	L	N	O	R	Z	C	Y	D	T	L
Y	A	X	N	W	J	X	Z	D	A	L	O	X	Y	F	Q	Z	X	E	W
Y	I	T	Y	W	A	G	G	E	D	M	O	L	W	Q	Y	X	J	A	K
T	Q	J	R	O	S	H	B	Q	B	D	B	P	E	W	B	Z	L	C	F
S	I	V	Q	L	S	A	F	Y	Y	G	C	A	E	A	W	R	S	H	X
R	W	R	R	I	N	Q	N	Q	X	I	S	S	Y	L	F	B	V	E	V
P	L	P	D	B	L	I	N	K	I	N	G	L	I	G	H	T	S	R	Y
B	I	G	G	E	S	T	P	W	F	A	R	A	W	A	Y	U	Z	E	H

Answer Key: *Dear Juno*

W	P					C		G	U			S					
P	A	E				R		R	N		O						
H			T	R		I		A	D				A				
O			C	S		S		S	N	E				R			
T	D			H	I	P		W	B	D	R			E			
O	U	R			E	M		I	A		M	N				D	
G	N		E		Y	D	M	N	C		O	E					
R	F			W	E		O	G	K		T	A					
A	O				L		N	I	Y				H	T			
P	L				L	E	S	N	A					E	H		
H	D				O		N	G	R						R		
	E				W		V		D					T			
C	D					E								T			
	A					L								E			
		T		W	A	G	G	E	D		O	L		A			
											P	E		C			
											E	A		H			
												F		E			
			B	L	I	N	K	I	N	G	L	I	G	H	T	S	R
B	I	G	G	E	S	T			F	A	R	A	W	A	Y		

Suggestion to Broaden Cultural Awareness:

We all have grandparents even if we do not interact with them. Relationship with the elderly is very important. How is the elderly treated in other cultures? What is adult-child relationship like? What are some cultures with nursing homes or other types of homes for the elderly?

Have the children choose a culture in which they would like to live. Take them to the library and have them choose books related to that culture. Have the children research the culture then write an imaginary letter to a "grandmother" in that culture. Combine the letters into a book and place the book in the classroom library.

Find out the possibility of writing to real adults (possibly in a nursing home in another country), or other children in another country. Help the children to start a pen-pal relationship with the adult or child of their choice.

Science

Activity #1   *Examine the Fish*

Skill: Sensory Experience (touch, see, smell)

Age/Grade Level: 4-6 Years

Book that can be used
with this project: McKissack, P. (1992). *Million Fish........More or Less*.
                               Illus: Dena Schutzer. New York: Alfred Knopf Publishers

Material: Fish
                               Implement (to be used to scale fish)
                               Paper towel
                               Large piece of plastic

Procedure:

1.   Place plastic on the table
2.   Place paper towel over plastic
3.   Place fish on paper towel and allow children to observe fish
4.   After children have had time to examine the fish
5.   Scale the fish

Activity #2   *Can You Put Me Back Together?*

Materials: Large outline of fish
                               Parts of a fish (cutouts - tail, fin, etc.)

Procedure: Have the children put the parts of the fish where they
                               belong.

Examine the Fish and *Can You Put Me Back Together*

Suggestion to Broaden Cultural Awareness:

If possible, take the children on a fishing trip. Before doing so, teach them about fishing gear. Also, take the children on a trip to the market to see the display of fish and purchase some types such as snapper, cod, etc. Afterwards have a "fish-fry" tasting party. Have the children experience fish prepared in different ways such as steamed, fried, escoveitched.

Make a concentration game of different types of fish (whale, shark, tuna, king, barracuda, grouper, snapper, catfish, bass, crappie, bluefish, pike and tarpon).

Activity:	*Dyeing With Plants*
Skill:	Obtaining/Using colors from plants
Age/Grade Level:	6 - 9 Years

There are numerous plants that can be used for dyeing in place of commercial dyes. Children will be delighted with the outcome of this type of activity.

Books that can be used
with this project:

Beskow, E. Pelle's New Suit. Illus: Elsa Beskow. New York: Harper Row Publishers.

Blood, C. & Link, M. (1976). *The Goat in the Rug.* Illus: Nancy Winslow Parker. New York: Four Winds Press.

dePaola, T. (1973). *Charlie Needs a Cloak.* Illus. Englewood, NJ: Prentice Hall.

dePaola, T. (1988). *Legend of the Indian Paintbrush.* Illus: New York: Scholastic, Inc.

Ziefert, H. (1986). *A New Coat for Anna.* Illus: Anita Lobel. New York: Alfred Knopf.

Materials:

Green	Leaves (crushed)
Yellow	onions or approximately nine to ten marigolds
Orange	carrot juice
Red	beet juice
Reddish blue	blueberries (crushed)
Tan	one teabag steeped in about eight ounces of hot water
Gold	powdered turmeric

Fabric:

(white) cotton
White yarn
Paintbrushes

Procedure:

To get the color green, crush **green** leaves and squish/squeeze in water or boil
     leaves to desired color.
For *yellow*, boil onions until desired color is attained.
Orange – grate carrots or puree in blender and strain.
Red – grate or boil beets. Add additional water if color is too bright.

     Have children experiment by dipping material in the different
     colors or use a paintbrush.

Suggestion to Broaden Cultural Awareness:

Plants are used for various things in different cultures. In some cultures plants
are worn, eaten or used for medicine. Have children research at least three cultures
where plants are worn such as Hawaii and some tribal communities in some countries
in Africa and South America. Have them check types of plants worn and the reasons.

Discuss some plants that we eat in the United States. Choose three of these
plants and put the names on a chart. Using Post-It notes have the children indicate on
the chart their favorite plant to eat. Make an age appropriate graph of their
preference.

The children can also interview persons from ethnic communities to find out
the types of plants that they eat. How are they similar or different to those that we
eat? Are they just different in name? Do they have the same name but look different?

Plants are also used for other purposes such as making dyes. Have the
children choose a culture and make an artifact related to the cultures (pottery, beads,
etc.). after it is completed, have them use dye made from plant to color the item.
Have the children compare colors from the dyes from plants with the colors from
commercial dyes.

Activity #1:	*Recycling Paper*

Skill:	Recycling
	Follow directions
	Fine motor

Age/Grade Level:	5-10 Years

Children need to know what recycling means. They also need to learn that we need to protect the environment and that saving trees is one way. Since paper is made from trees, children can do their part by recycling paper.

Books that can be used
with this project:
Cherry, L. (1992). *A River Ran Wild: An Environmental History*. Illus: Lynne Cherry. New York: Harcourt Brace Jovanovich, Publishers.

Cherry, L. (1990). *The Great Kapok Tree*. Illus: Lynne Cherry. New York: Gulliver Books.

Materials:
Tub or bucket for soaking paper
Blender
Water
Towel (for clean up)
Newspaper and other soft types of paper
2 paper making screens - approximately 12"x 12"
Poster with recycle symbol - Reduce, Reuse, Recycle
Glue
Markers and crayons, glitter, dried flowers, etc.

Procedure:

1. Tear paper into very small pieces and put in tub
2. Cover the paper with water
3. Use hand to scrunch paper (or use blender to make mushy)
4. Leave the paper to soak in the water overnight
5. To m make paper, put the mushy pulp on one screen
6. Place the other screen on top of the pulp and squeeze out the water
7. Place the screens, with the pulp, in a place to dry. Leave it overnight
8. When the paper is dry, remove the screens
9. Allow children to decorate the new paper.

Activity #2:   *Recycle Other Items*

Skill: Collect and classify items for recycling
                        Categorize and sort items by their attributes

Age/Grade Level: 5-10 Years

Books that can be used
with this project: Cherry, L. (1992). *A River Ran Wild: An Environmental
                        History*. Illus: Lynne Cherry. New York: Harcourt
                        Brace Jovanovich, Publishers.

                        Cherry, L. (1990). *The Great Kapok Tree*. Illus: Lynne
                        Cherry. New York: Gulliver Books.

Materials: Various items for sorting (see below)

Procedure:

1.   Have children bring in a variety of items
2.   Have children sort items into bio- and non biodegradable groups
3.   Have children check items for recycle symbol and sort items that can be
      recycled

Examples of Items to be sorted:

Aluminum cans	Cardboard
Wire	Packing materials
Paper products	Styrofoam - cups
Popsicle sticks	Various cans
Plastic - bottles, toys, etc.	Pencils and pens
Scrap paper	Grocery bags - plastic and paper
Egg cartons	Yarn

To recycle clothing see tie dyeing

Suggestion to Broaden Cultural Awareness:

Protecting the environment is a global issue. Children need to learn that what is done in one culture impacts other cultures. Discuss the recycling symbol with the children. Also discuss the three "Rs" (Recycle, Reduce and Reuse), and the meaning of biodegradable. Take the children on a field trip to a recycling plant so they can see what happens to recycling material.

Do a project with the children. Put soil in a container and "plant" items that are degradable and non-degradable.(for example, plastic, paper, soda cans, green leaves, natural food items, etc.).

Give each child a 5x8 index card. Instruct them to list on their card five or six things they can do, as individuals, to protect the environment. For example, become involved in a recycling project and sort items that can be recycled.

Have the children research what some other countries are doing to protect the environment. Do they recycle? Do they also have a symbol to assist people in understanding what can be recycled? Have them put their findings on a website.

Activity: *Crossword Puzzle*

Skill: Complete Crossword Puzzle
                       Increase vocabulary
                       Dictionary use

Age/Grade Level: 7-10 Years

Book that can be used
with this project: Brisson, P. (1998). *The Summer My Father Was Ten.*
                       Illus: Andrea Shine. Pennsylvania: Boyds Mills Press.

On the following page is a crossword puzzle which relates to the above story. Use the clues listed to help you find the words for the puzzle. When you are through, use the Answer key to check your answers.

Title: *The Summer My Father Was Ten*

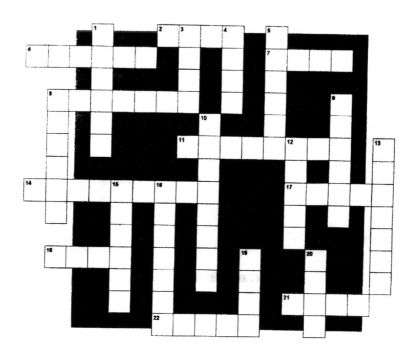

WEED, BOUQUET, GROW, TRUDGE, OPERA, THUMP, PULP, TRAMPLE, RUIN, RAKE, SMOOTH, STAMMER, MESS, BLOOM, TOMATO, VEGETABLE, UPROOT, PICK, WARM, GARDEN, NEIGHBOR, TROWEL, REMEMBER

Crossword Puzzle

Definitions: *The Summer My Father Was Ten*

Across

2) to increase in size, amount or length

6) to tear or pull up by the roots

7) a dirty or disorderly condition; untidy group of things

8) to step on heavily and crush

11) a person who lives near by

14) a plant used for food

17) a play in which all or most of the words are sung

18) a plant that is useless or harmful or grows where it is not wanted

21) to select; collect

22) a dull, heavy sound

Down

1) a juicy, red berry

3) a tool that has a long handle with teeth or prongs attached at one end

4) somewhat hot; not cold

5) having a surface that is not uneven or rough

8) a tool with a flat blade that is used for spreading and smoothing wet plaster, cement or a similar substance

9) a piece of ground where flowers or vegetables are grown

10) have something come into the mind again

12) the flower of a plant

13) to speak or say with difficulty

15) to walk slowly and with effort

16) a bunch of flowers

19) the soft, juicy part of fruits and vegetables

20) destruction, damage or collapse

Crossword Puzzle

Answers: *The Summer My Father Was Ten*

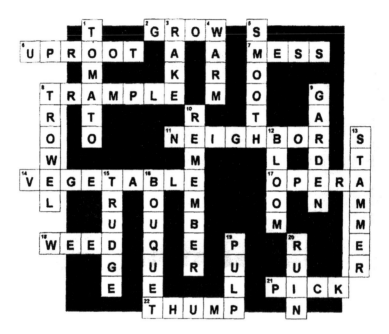

WEED, BOUQUET, GROW, TRUDGE, OPERA, THUMP, PULP, TRAMPLE,
RUIN, RAKE, SMOOTH, STAMMER, MESS, BLOOM, TOMATO, VEGETABLE,
UPROOT, PICK, WARM, GARDEN, NEIGHBOR, TROWEL, REMEMBER

Suggestion to Broaden Cultural Awareness:

In this story and activity children learn the importance of taking responsibility for their actions. We need to respect others and, in so doing, show respect for ourselves. We also need to accept the wisdom of the elderly and respect them for their contributions.

Different cultures have a different standard for pragmatics. On a six pieces of posterboard or oaktag (approximately 2"x1 1/2" write the following words/phrases in Italian, Spanish and French (one on each card) "hello, goodbye, please, thank you, good morning, goodnight." laminate and put velcro on the back of each.

On a piece of posterboard titled: "We Speak Other Languages," write across the top English, Italian, Spanish and French. List each of the above words under "English" on the left side. The children will them match the Italian, Spanish and French words/phrases to the English version.

Be sure to provide an *Answer Key*.

Activity: *Making Tortillas*

Skill: Prepare ethnic food
                       Measuring
                       Follow directions

Age/Grade Level: 5-10 Years

Wheat flour tortilla is a basic food in Northern Mexico (Corn is used in central and southern Mexico). Below is a recipe for making tortillas.

Book that can be used
with this project: Paulsen, G. (1995). *The Tortilla Factory*. Illus: Ruth Wright Paulsen. New York: Voyager Books.

Materials:

3 cups   processed cornmeal or unbleached flour (Masaharina or *Maseca labels)
1/3 cup   vegetable oil or shortening
1 cup   water
Large griddle or skillet (preferably iron where the heat distributes more evenly)

Procedure:

1.   Mix the Masaharina or Maseca and vegetable oil
2.   Add water
3.   Make small balls
4.   Place on lightly floured table and roll out into thin, flat circles
5.   Heat griddle or skillet
6.   Place tortilla circles on griddle or skillet and brown each side
7.   Serve with butter (or fried beans)

* Maseca usually works better

Making Tortillas

Suggestion to Broaden Cultural Awareness:

We all need food in order to survive. However, each culture has its own staples. To help children appreciate another way to experience cultural diversity, they should be encouraged to try different ethnic foods.

Preparing and enjoying foods from other cultures is another way to help children appreciate ethnic diversity. The tortilla is the Mexican version of "flatbreads" such as pita bread which Southern Mexicans refer to as "Arab bread." Take the children on a field trip to an ethnic food store (preferably a Barrio) to shop for the items to make the tortillas. Before going, have them research information on making tortillas.

Provide the children with the opportunity to taste different types of bread from different cultures and compare tastes. For example, Italian bread. Irish soda bread, Swedish rye, Challah twisted egg bread which is Jewish and Jamaican hard dough bread. (Use Post-It notes on a chart to show preferences)

Have children interview people from different cultures and find out the names of foods that are popular in that culture. For example gyros and baklava from Greece, hot dogs and hamburgers in the United States, different types of pasta dishes from Italy and Kugel noodle pudding which is Jewish. A discussion of taste, with which they may or may not be familiar, as well as the culture from which the food is derived, will help children appreciate differences.

Activity: *Baking Sweet Potato Pudding*

Skill: Measuring
Follow written directions
Observe changes (taking place in foods)

Age/Grade Level: 5-10 Years

Sweet potato is enjoyed in many cultures. The potato can be cooked, roasted or baked. Below is the recipe for baking a sweet potato pudding.

Book that can be used
with this project: Grifalconi, A. (1986). *The Village of Round and Square Houses*. Illus: Ann Grifalconi. Boston: Little, Brown and Company.

Materials:

4	eggs
2 cups	milk
3 cups	grated, uncooked, sweet potatoes (use sweet potatoes which are white inside. These can be found in Korean or West Indian stores)
2 cups	brown sugar
4 tablespoons	melted butter
1 teaspoon	cinnamon
2 teaspoons	vanilla
2 tablespoons	raisins (optional)

Procedure:

1.   Beat eggs slightly
2.   Add other ingredients together in blender. Mix well.
3.   Pour into greased baking dish
4.   Bake for 40 minutes at 350 degrees F. Serve warm or cold.

Suggestion to Broaden Cultural Awareness:

Discuss with children how food changes. Alert them to the changes that take place during the grating, mixing and baking process. Talk about the ingredients and compare and contrast those from different countries. Discuss nutritional value. Finally, compare to sweet potato pie made from yams.

Engage children in a "smelling" activity. Place a different powered spice such as vanilla, cinnamon, nutmeg, paprika, cloves, pimento, allspice in different film canisters. Cover with porous material such as cheesecloth. Put the names of all the items on a chart. Place children in groups and have them smell the container and guess what it contains.

Do the same activity for items that can be safely tasted.

Have groups of children research where some of these spices originated. For example, pimento, nutmeg and paprika.

Activity: *Making A Volcano*

Skill: Follow directions; Measuring;
                       Mixing ingredients

Age/Grade Level: 6-10 Years

Children should find this activity very interesting especially when the volcano erupts

Book that can be used
with this project: Grifalconi, A. (1986). *The Village of Round and Square
                       Houses*. Illus: Ann Grifalconi. Boston: Little, Brown and
                       Company.

Materials:

1 Tablespoon	baking soda
1 Tablespoon	vinegar
3 Cups	flour
3/4 Cup	salt
½ Teaspoon	oil
2-3 Drops	red and yellow food coloring (for lava)
Water	as needed
	Liquid dishwashing soap
1	Empty toilet tissue roll or plastic jar or clean frozen juice can.
1	Plastic paper plate

Procedure:

1. Add the flour, salt and oil to some water and mix
2. Add more water as needed to make dough
3. Put tissue roll (plastic jar or juice can) in the center of a large plastic picnic plate to make open crater for volcano
4. Use dough to make cone around the tissue roll (jar or frozen juice can)
5. Put baking soda in the tube
6. Add soap and the red and yellow food coloring
7. Add vinegar - this will make the volcano erupt

* Before adding vinegar, ask children what they think will happen.

N. B.   *This is a messy activity. Cover table with plastic and have young
         children wear a smock.*

Suggestion to Broaden Cultural Awareness:

There is much more the children can learn about volcanoes. For example, children can research major volcanoes such as the volcano on Mount Vesuvius and the one on Mount St Helen. Children can also research dormant and active volcanoes for example where some of them are located. They can also research recently erupted volcanoes such as Etna in Italy which erupted in November 2002. They can also research volcanoes in the United States, for example, the volcano in Yellowstone, which erupted in January 1998 and a volcano in Long Valley, California, which erupted in April 1996.

Children can also research how volcanoes impact the lives of residents when they have erupted and even when they are dormant. Have the children also discuss why they believe it is so difficult for people to leave an are when a volcano has erupted. If they could, what would they advise people to do when a volcano first erupts?

Math

Activity: *Fruit/Vegetable Sorting*

Skill: Classify and sort according to specific attributes
                                   Identifying fruits and vegetables

Age/Grade Level: 4-6 Years

Book that can be used
with this project: Kimmel, E. (1988). *Anansi and the Moss-Covered
                                   Rock*. Illus: Janet Stevens. New York: Holiday House.

Materials:

Various fruits and vegetables (or pictures of fruits and vegetables) such as:

Avocado	Carrots
Banana	Broccoli
Cantaloupe	Celery
Papaya	Cucumber
Kiwi	Radish
Tangelos	Lettuce
Mango	Peas
Raspberries	Strawberries

Procedure:

1.   Lay fruits and vegetables on a table
2.   Have one side of chart paper labeled "Fruit" and the other side
     "Vegetable"
3.   Have children put items under the correct label

Activity #2	*Fruit/Vegetable Tasting Party*

Skill:
Tasting and selecting favorite fruits and vegetables
Develop and interpret graphs
Sensory (touch, taste and smell)

Age/Grade Level:
4-6 Years

Book that can be used
with this project:
Kimmel, E. (1988). *Anansi and the Moss-Covered Rock.* Illus: Janet Stevens. New York: Holiday House.

Materials:
Fruits and vegetables

Procedure:

Put chart paper on the wall
Have children taste fruit and vegetables
Have children put sticky notes under their favorite fruit and vegetables
Tally totals on graph

Suggestion to Broaden Cultural Awareness:

On a chart put the following labels: sour, sweet, bitter. Use pictures or drawings of the face to depict what the face looks like when tasting these foods. Ask the children to taste each of the fruits and then identify and describe each of the fruits they taste. Ask them which ones they like and which ones they do not like and also explain why they like or dislike each fruit or vegetable.

Discuss the texture and nutritional value of fruits. Also discuss the cultures from which the fruits originated.

Note: Try to provide a wide variety of fruits and vegetables that originate from different cultures (e.g. papaya, pomegranate, kiwi, guinep, guava, apples, etc.).

Activity:	*Making A Dream Catcher*
Skill:	Fine motor development Eye-hand coordination
Age/Grade Level:	6-10 Years
Book that can be used with this project:	Osofsky, A. (1992). *Dream Catcher*. Illus: Ed Young. New York: Orchard Books.
Materials:	Small plastic circle (pliable twig or metal will substitute) Leather string Dental floss Feathers Small beads

Procedure:

1. Weave dental floss across plastic ring. Make knot at cross sections to form a web.
2. Attach one bead to inside of web
3. Wrap circle with leather string (covering plastic)
4. Attach leather string with beads and feather to bottom
5. Attach leather string with loop at the top for hanging

Suggestion to Broaden Cultural Awareness:

In many cultures there are rituals to help children enjoy the peacefulness and safety of sleep. The "boogeyman" exists in many cultures. However, different cultures use different strategies to protect them from the "boogeyman". In the Ojibway tribe the Dream Catcher is used to catch children's bad dreams.

Have children interview persons from different cultures to find out the name of their "boogeyman" and what method is used to ensure children feel safe and sound when they go to sleep. That is, how are children are protected from the "boogeyman".

Activity #1:   *Weaving – Wall Hanging*

Skill: Fine motor development
                           Eye-hand coordination
                           Follow directions

Age/Grade Level: 6-10 Years

Book that can be used
with this project: Blood, C. & Link, M. (1976). *The Goat in the Rug*. Illus:
                           Nancy Winslow Parker. New York: Four Winds Press.

Materials: 2 pieces of dowel, each one foot long
                           6-8 pieces of yarn 12 inches long
                           Fabric strips 1/4"x 12 inches
                           Cotton strips at least 12 inches long
                           Yarn 12 inches long
                           Twine – different sizes and colors
                           Colored feathers

Procedure:

1.   Lay the dowel one above the other.
2.   Tie one end of each piece of yarn on the top dowel and complete by tying
     the other end on the dowel below (to form loom)
3.   After all pieces have been tied, forming a loom - have children put yarn,
     twine, fabric and cotton strips horizontally
4.   Decorate with feathers

Activity #2:	*Weaving*

Skill:	Fine motor development
	Eye-hand coordination
	Follow directions

Age/Grade Level:	6-10 Years

Book that can be used with the project:	Blood, C. & Link, M. (1976). *The Goat in the Rug.* Illus: Nancy Winslow Parker. New York: Four Winds Press.

Materials:	8 ½ " piece of poster board
	Hole punch
	8 Pieces of yarn 12 inches long
	Fabric strips, cotton strips, twine (12 inches long and in different colors)
	Colored feathers

Procedure:

1. Punch 7-8 holes an inch apart ½ an inch at top and bottom of posterboard
2. Run yarn through hole at top and bottom and tie (to form loom)
3. Weave yarn, twine, fabric strips and cotton strips horizontally through hanging yarn
4. Decorate with feathers.

Suggestion to Broaden Cultural Awareness:

Rugs and mats are used in many cultures. There are rugs and mats made from straw, raffia and rags. The use of rugs and mats is culturally defined. Basically, for climatic reasons, some cultures may be more inclined to use straw mats while other cultures may be more inclined to use oriental rugs.

For example, the oriental rug which is made from natural fibre such as wool, cotton or silk are very popular in Europe, Asia and the United States. This type of rug is usually made in countries such as Iran, India and China.

If possible take the children to a department store where they can see actual oriental rugs. Also, show them pictures of oriental rugs and rugs made by the Navajo so they can compare. Point out that the Navajo design is peculiar to the particular weaver so each is very different.

Have the children research different types of rugs and mats and how they are made. To introduce the children to weaving have them make mats from strips of colored construction paper.

Have someone who knows how to spin/weave cotton take a cotton gin to your classroom and demonstrate spinning for the children.

Use a world map and mark Window Rock in the United States as well as places such as China, India and Iran. This will allow the children to see that we trade with places that are far away.

Refer to *Abuela's Weave*

Activity: *Seed Collage*

Skill: Fine motor development
Eye-hand coordination
Figure-ground development

Age/Grade Level: 5-7 years

Book that can be used
with this project: Fleishman, P. (1997). *Seedfolks*. Illus: Judy Pedersen.
New York: Joanna Coulter Books/Harper Trophy.

Materials: Construction paper
Variety of Seeds
Glue

Procedure:

1.   Have children draw design on paper
2.   Children can then select seeds they will use
3.   Have children put glue on area with design
4.   Children should then place seeds on glued area
5.   Leave to dry

Note: This activity should be closely supervised

Activity #2:	*Sorting Seeds According to Specific Attributes*
Skill:	Fine motor development Sorting/classifying (color, size, etc.)
Age/Grade Level:	4-6 Years.
Book that can be used with this project:	Fleishman, P. (1997). *Seedfolks.* Illus: Judy Pedersen New York: Joanna Coulter Books/Harper Trophy.
Materials:	Have available various types of seeds
Procedure:	Have the children sort the seeds.

Suggestion to Broaden Cultural Awareness:

In some cultures, the idea of sharing is a very important. People automatically share what they have with others. Sharing and cooperation are important aspects of the human experience but are very difficult concepts for children to grasp.

In this story the people shared, were cooperative and supported each other with the project. Discuss with the children the importance of sharing. Also, discuss with them how when the attitude of the gardeners changed, the gardening project began to be more successful. Help them see that it was the fact that everyone was involved and cared for each other that helped to make the project successful.

To support the idea of sharing, have a planting activity. Select seeds such red beans, black eyed peas and lima beans. Put the children in groups of three or four. Within the groups children take on different responsibilities such as watering, measuring and keeping notes on growth, etc. Discuss with them what is likely to happen if people do not do what they are supposed to do. They then see how important it is to cooperate with each other.

Ask the children to come up with strategies one might use to get others to cooperate or take responsibility for their action when they don't. Also ask them what their parents do when they do not share or do their chores.

Note: This activity should be closely supervised.

Activity: *Crossword Puzzle*

Skill: Complete crossword puzzle
                             Increase vocabulary
                             Increase/develop dictionary skill

Age/Grade Level: 7-19 Years

Book that can be used
with this project: Pinkney, G. J. (1992). *Back Home*. Illus: Jerry Pinkney.
                             New York: Dial books for Young Readers.

Ernestine had a wonderful time visiting relatives on the farm in North Carolina. Complete the following crossword puzzle using the words selected from the above story. First try to get the meaning of the words from the story. Use the dictionary to assist you.

When you are through, use the completed puzzle to check your answer.

Title: *Back Home*

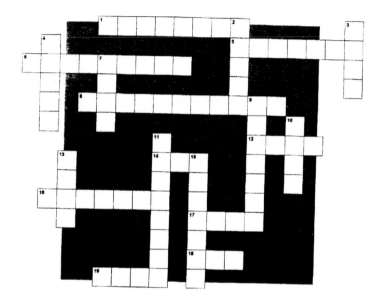

PLATFORM, DEPOT, GOAT, WARM, GRIP, CRINKLE, SCENT, PLOW,
OVERALLS, BARN, LAG, DILAPIDATED, SHY, ENGRAVE, BOUQUET,
HEAP, RECOGNIZE, GLIMPSE, MULE

Crossword Puzzle

Definitions:

Across	Down

Across

1) loose-fitting trousers

5) to form or cause to form wrinkles or ripples; wrinkle; cripple

6) to know and remember from before; identify

8) fallen into ruin or decay; broken down

12) an animal that has two horns and a beard

14) to delay; to fall behind the others

16) a bunch of flowers

17) an animal that is the offspring of a female horse and a male donkey

18) to be bashful and not forthcoming

19) somewhat hot; not cold

Down

2) smell

3) a collection of things piled together

4) a railroad or bus terminal

7) a firm hold; tight grasp

9) to cut or carve letters, figures, or designs into a surface

10) a farm building used for storage of animals, tools and food

11) a raised, flat surface

13) a heavy farm tool for cutting through and turning over soil

15) a quick look; glance

Answers:

Back Home

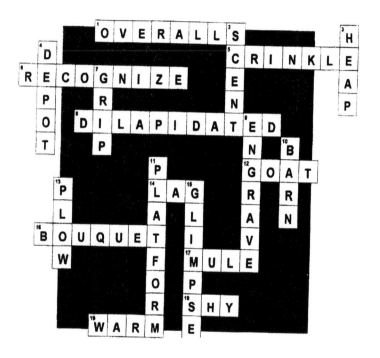

PLATFORM, DEPOT, GOAT, WARM, GRIP, CRINKLE, SCENT, PLOW, OVERALLS, BARN, LAG, DILAPIDATED, SHY, ENGRAVE, BOUQUET, HEAP, RECOGNIZE, GLIMPSE, MULE

Suggestion to Broaden Cultural Awareness:

Make a concentration game of people, animals and equipment found on a farm. Include pigs, sheep and goats as well as animals that would be farm animals in other cultures. For objects include hoe, fork, rake and wheel barrow.

For the people on the farm, use people representing different ethnic groups so children will be aware that farming takes place across all cultures and with all races.

Social Studies

Activity: *Word Search*

Skill: Figure-ground (locating words)
                                           Follow directions (find specific words among random
                                           letters)

Age/Grade Level: 7-10 Years

Book that can be used
with this project: Castaneda, O. S. (1993). *Abuela's Weave*. Illus: Enrique
                                           O. Sanchez. New York: Lee & Low Publishers, Inc.

In the grid on the following page are the words which are listed below along with some random letters. All the words are from the story. Find and circle the listed words.

When you are through, check your answer on the completed grid

| Word List |

1.	JOLT	11.	BIRTHMARK
2.	THREADS	12.	RUMOR
3.	THRUST	13.	GRUFFY
4.	WEAVE	14.	SUNSET
5.	BACKSTRAP	15.	DISGUISED
6.	LOOM	16.	SHAWL
7.	COMPOUND	17.	MOURNING
8.	THATCH	18.	INTRICATE
9.	TAPESTRIES	19.	ANCESTORS
10.	TEASE	20.	FUMES

Title: *Abuela's Weave*

S	R	D	V	J	H	O	R	B	N	G	B	S	V	E	N	P	O	Y	T
A	U	Q	I	C	J	O	P	E	A	C	I	H	B	S	G	C	I	N	J
J	T	N	S	S	L	P	V	S	C	S	R	A	U	A	J	Y	Q	R	R
E	E	S	S	X	G	P	Y	A	B	G	T	W	O	G	Q	L	S	G	F
M	A	W	Q	E	P	U	I	P	R	T	H	L	V	Q	Z	N	I	T	B
O	S	X	Z	J	T	E	I	J	F	I	M	R	C	L	F	L	D	Y	N
U	E	F	U	M	E	S	I	S	B	D	A	U	T	C	C	A	H	U	E
R	G	K	A	C	L	H	P	M	E	R	R	Z	H	C	T	X	O	G	X
N	A	N	C	E	S	T	O	R	S	D	K	R	R	M	H	P	A	F	O
I	W	E	A	V	E	U	K	H	H	W	W	C	E	X	J	K	F	N	F
N	I	N	T	R	I	C	A	T	E	Z	F	E	A	R	U	M	O	R	X
G	T	B	G	E	J	S	A	Y	E	X	C	G	D	L	U	X	T	J	F
D	H	A	Z	T	L	O	R	Q	A	M	O	C	S	D	W	Y	J	P	A
C	A	C	K	I	O	Z	L	B	T	G	K	Y	O	G	R	U	F	F	Y
W	T	K	B	S	O	F	F	T	B	A	C	Q	G	M	N	J	J	T	Y
V	C	S	L	L	M	V	V	N	Z	B	X	O	S	O	P	N	L	D	R
M	H	T	J	O	R	T	P	B	T	C	N	U	C	S	O	O	X	B	D
P	G	R	V	I	J	X	K	A	F	Q	K	I	L	Z	G	X	U	I	Q
X	G	A	M	T	T	S	U	F	N	G	T	H	R	U	S	T	Q	N	W
B	J	P	G	T	A	P	E	S	T	R	I	E	S	T	W	O	X	X	D

Answers: *Abuela's Weave*

1	2	3	4	5	6	7	8	9	10	11	12	13	14	15	16	17	18	19
S		D									B	S						
	U		I								I	H						
	T	N		S							R	A						
	E		S		G						T	W						
M	A			E		U					H	L						
O	S				T		I				M							
U	E	F	U	M	E	S		S			A		T					
R								E			R		H					
N	A	N	C	E	S	T	O	R	S	D	K		R					
I	W	E	A	V	E								E					
N	I	N	T	R	I	C	A	T	E				A	R	U	M	O	R
G	T	B		J									D					
	H	A		L	O					C	S		S					
	A	C			O		L					O	G	R	U	F	F	Y
	T	K			O		T						M					
	C	S			M									P				
	H	T													O			
	R															U		
	A										T	H	R	U	S	T		N
	P		T	A	P	E	S	T	R	I	E	S						D

Suggestion to Broaden Cultural Awareness:

Weaving is an activity that is done in many cultures in different forms. Although some items are woven by machine, many items are still done manually, usually using a variety of tools.

To expose children to some of the tools used for weaving, make a concentration game of some of the tools used for weaving. Get twenty pieces of poster board 2"x11/2." get two pictures of each of the following, glue to poster board and laminate:

cotton balls	spindle
cotton plant	whorl
loom (backstrap or other type)	carding combs
tapestry	battens
shears	dye bucket

Children will turn pictures face down on the table and pick up and try to match as many pairs as possible. The person who remembers where pictures are located and makes the most matches is the winner.

Teach the children to count from one to twenty in Spanish then create a simple Spanish Bingo. Put Spanish number/name (***uno dos, tres***, etc.), on one side and the Arabic numbers (1-20) on the other.

Refer to the following:

Activity:	*Comparing two Stories*
Activity:	*Weaving – Wall Hanging*
Activity:	*Weaving*

Activity:	*All About Me Book*
Skill:	Fine motor development Eye-hand coordination Develop sense of self Recognize that spoken word can be written down
Age/Grade Level:	5-10 Years
Books that can be used with this project:	Adoff, A. (1973). *Black Is Brown is Tan.* Illus: Emily Arnold McCully. New York: Harper Trophy. Hamanaka, S. (1994). *All the Colors of the Earth.* Illus: Sheila Hamanaka. New York: Morrow Junior Books. Hoffman, M. (1990). *Amazing Grace.* Illus: Caroline Binch. New York: Dial Books. Hudson, C. & Ford, B. *Bright Eyes, Brown Skin.* Illus: George Ford. Orange, New Jersey: Just Us Books.

Materials:

Sheets of plain newsprint (enough to make a book)
Ten special items (brought by each child)
Polaroid or digital camera
Glue, crayons, markers and glitter

Procedure:

1. Take a picture of each child
2. Have the child glue picture to the front of the book
3. Have them write their names on the cover
4. Have children glue items to each page in their book
5. Have them dictate a story about each page
6. Children can then decorate the cover and pages with glitter and markers.

Activity: *Who Am I?*

Skill: Cooperation
                                   Making choices
                                   Following directions

Age/Grade Level: 6-10 Years

Books that can be used
with this project: Cannon, J. *Stellaluna*. Illus: Janell Cannon. New York:
                                   Harcourt Brace and Co.

                                   Carle, E. (1984). *The Mixed-Up Chameleon*. Illus: Eric
                                   Carle. New York: Harper Trophy.

                                   Guarino, D. (1989). *Is Your Mama A Llama*? Illus: Steven
                                   Kellog. New York: Scholastic, Inc.

                                   Hoffman, M. (191990). *Amazing Grace*. Illus: Caroline
                                   Binch. New York: Dial Books for Young Readers.

                                   Nikola, L. (1994). *Bein' With You This Way*. Illus:
                                   Michael Bryant. New York: Lee and Low Books.

Materials:

In groups of four – have children choose an ethnic group or culture and bring in at least three items/information from that culture (for example, clothing from an ethnic group or pictures if actual clothing not available)

Procedure:

In this activity children become aware that though different, people in most cultures do wear clothing and the clothing is culture defined.

1.   Have children sit in teams (to assist each other)
2.   Have children show and share items country/culture of origin
3.   Allow points for originality, knowledge and presentation
4.   Now put all the clothing together.
5.   Pull different items and see if children can recall information (they can assist each other).
6.   Group that can identify the most items is the winner.

Suggestion to Broaden Cultural Awareness:

How people dress is an important part of their culture. However, when people are seen in traditional dress this is sometimes confused with everyday wear. It is important to point out that people from a variety of cultures wear clothes similar to what we wear in the United States but do dress differently for a variety of reasons, usually on special occasions . However, do point out that traditional dress is not a costume.

We can help children become aware of different types of traditional dress. Make a book of pictures of children from different cultures such as Greek, Scottish, Spanish, Indian, Hawaiian, Chinese, Vietnamese, Nigerian and any two Native American tribes, in traditional dress. Below each picture put a piece of velcro. Type and laminate the name of each country represented and place in an envelope (put velcro on the back of each). Have the children match the name of the culture represented by putting the correct name below.

Be sure to provide an *Answer Key*.

Activity: *Synonyms*

Skill: Recognizing words that express similar meaning
                                    Matching words with similar meaning
                                    Figure-ground (locating words among random letters)

Age/Grade Level: 7-10 Years

Book that can be used
with this project: Bunting, E. (1994). *A Day's Work*. Illus: Ronald Himler.
                                    New York: Clarion Books.

On the following page is a list of words. In the section marked "Across" and "Down," on page 114, you will find words with similar meaning. Find the match for the words from the list and put them in the grid.

When you are through, check your answer in the completed grid.

Title: *A Day's Work*

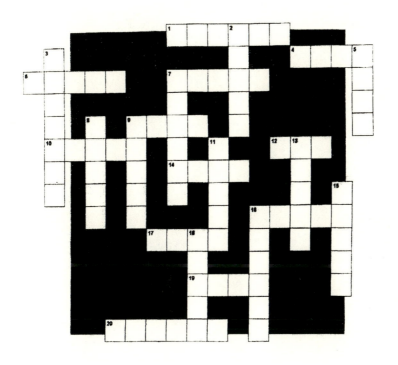

SLOW, COLD, EARLY, SKINNY, DART, THICK, OMEN, TILT, URGENT,
TOUGH, PUSH, SLOPE, CLIMB, SMELL, CLUMP, PROWL, SPLASH,
LOOSE, STARE, WHISPER, QUIVER, SAD, ANGER

Title: *A Day's Work*

Across	**Down**
1) immediate	2) beforehand
4) bolt	3) hushed tones
6) dense	5) slant
7) gaze	7) splatter
9) chilly	8) unrestrained
10) sneak	9) cluster
12) rueful	11) strong
14) gradual	13) rage
16) scent	15) mounting
17) shove	16) thin
19) sign	18) hillside
20) shake	

Synonyms

Answers: *A Day's Work*

SLOW, COLD, EARLY, SKINNY, DART, THICK, OMEN, TILT, URGENT,
TOUGH, PUSH, SLOPE, CLIMB, SMELL, CLUMP, PROWL, SPLASH,
LOOSE, STARE, WHISPER, QUIVER, SAD, ANGER

Suggestion to Broaden Cultural Awareness:

Collect pictures of various types of hats used for occupation, weather and religion (for example, sombrero, fedora, beret, dibiri, fugulan, yarmulke, Panama hat, and turban). Put the pictures of each of the hats on the left side of a poster board. Attach a string that can be extended from each picture to the other side. On the other side write the name of the type of hat (out of order). Beside each put a brad. Have children match the type of hat to its name by running the string from the hat to name of the type of hat and wrapping it around the brad.

Provide an *Answer Key*.

Note: To extend the activity, add the culture, occupation or religion associated with the particular hat.

Activity: *Making Bracelet – Clay Beads*

Skill: Eye-hand coordination (visual motor development)
Fine motor
Mixing colors
Measuring

Age/Grade Level: 5-10 Years

Book that can be used
with this project: Uchida, Y. (1993). *The Bracelet*. Illus: Joanna Yardley.
New York: The Putnam and Grosset Group.

Materials:

1 cup cornstarch
2 cups baking soda
1 1/4 cup cold water
Food coloring
Glitter
Pipe cleaners or thread

Procedure:

1.   Mix the cornstarch and baking soda
2.   Add the water
3.   Cook and stir over medium heat for four minutes
4.   Let mixture cool
5.   Add glitter, food coloring, etc., to decorate
6.   Form very small beads from the mixture
7.   Punch a small hole through the center of each ball
8.   Bake at 300 degrees for forty five minutes or leave in the sun for about
two days
9.   String together using thread or pipe cleaners.

Activity: Paper Chain Bracelet

Skill: Fine motor
Eye-hand coordination
Sequencing
Name abstract position (first, second, etc.)
Match patterns
Identify colors

Age/Grade Level: 5-7 Years

Book that can be used
with this project: Uchida, Y. (1993). *The Bracelet*. Illus: Joanna Yardley.
New York: The Putnam and Grosset Group.

Materials:

Strips of colored construction (or other colored paper,
leather or cloth) 2"x 3/4"
Needle and thread or glue

Procedure:

1.   Put strips together in patterned sequence to make chain (e.g. orange, red, yellow)
2.   Glue or sew strips
3.   Make long enough to fit child's wrist
4.   Discuss pattern with the children (e.g. Which color is first? Which is next to the red? etc.)

Note: Dyed macaroni can also be strung together for beads.

Suggestion to Broaden Cultural Awareness:

Friendship is a universal facet of life. However, we lose friends as well as things we love. In this activity children learn how we can maintain memories of friendship through "keepsakes."

Have children bring in keepsakes they have gotten. Take pictures of the items and put the pictures on a chart and label them. Make a photo album type book of the items. Allow each child a page beside his/her entry to write about the item and what it means to him/her. Also allow the children to decorate their page if they want to do so. Keep the book in the classroom library.

Now have the children interview friends or relatives from other cultures and find out what they have given or received as keepsakes. This will expose children to a variety of cultural gift items. Have them get pictures, if possible. Put together in another interesting book: ***"Keepsakes From Around the World."***

Activity: *Making Potato Pancakes (Latkes)*

Skill: Prepare and try ethnic food
                                        Mix ingredients

Age/Grade Level: 5-7 Years

Books that can be used
with this project: Groner, J. & Wikler, M. (1990). *All About Hanukkah.* Illus: Rosalyn Schanzer. New York: Gryphon House.

Kimmel, E. (1988). *The Chanukah Guest.* Illus: Giora Carmi. New York: Scholastic, Inc.

Manushkin, F. (1997). *The Matzah That Papa Brought Home.* Illus: Ned Bittinger. New York: Scholastic, Inc.

Potato pancake (latke) is a popular Jewish food. Use the recipe below to make latkes, similar to those made by Bubba Brayna.

Materials:

6-8 medium potatoes (peeled)
2 large eggs, beaten
½ cup flour (or matzo or mafzah meal)
1 medium onion
1 teaspoon salt
Vegetable oil as needed
Skillet (preferably iron - heat distributes more evenly)

Making Potato Pancakes (Latkes)

Procedure

1.   Peel and grate potatoes
2.   Grate onions
3.   Add grated onions to grated potatoes
4.   Squeeze out excess liquid
5.   Place in medium sized bowl
6.   Beat eggs and add to mixture in bowl
7.   Add flour and salt
8.   Mix all ingredients
9.   Heat one inch of oil in skillet until very hot
10. Pour spoonfuls of batter onto skillet for 6 - 8 minutes. Make sure each side is golden brown and crisp.
11. Flip over and do the same for the other side
12. Place on paper towels to drain excess oil

Suggestion to Broaden Cultural Awareness:

Food is a very important part of culture. We have everyday types of food but certain foods also are used for certain celebrations. Ask the children to identify some celebrations and the foods associated with them. For example, in the United States, turkey meat is usually eaten during Thanksgiving and Christmas celebrations.

The potato is used in many forms in a variety of cultures. In the United States, potato dishes include potato hash (hash browns), mashed potatoes, baked potatoes, potato pie, french fries and potato chips. Is the potato used in other ways in other countries. The children can choose four to five cultures and in groups research if and how potatoes are use. They can also find out if the potato is home grown or imported.

Activity #1:	*What Do I see?*

Skill:	Fine motor development
	Develop positive self concept
	Identify/Choose colors

Age/Grade Level:	5 – 10 Years

Book that can be used to	
support this project:	Ginsburg, M. (1988). *The Chinese Mirror*. Illus: Margot Zemach. New York: Harcourt Brace Jovanovich.

Materials:

    Mirror
    Construction paper
    Crayons and markers

Procedure:

1. Give each child a mirror
2. Have the child draw a picture of what he or she sees in the mirror
3. Put the pictures together in a book titled "Our Album."
4. Put the book in the classroom library.

Activity #2:   *Mirror Game*

Skill: Imitate fine/large motor movement
                                Match numbers
                                Recognize numbers 1-5
                                Follow directions

Age/Grade Level: 5-10 Years

Book that can be used to
support this project: Ginsburg, M. (1988). *The Chinese Mirror*. Illus: Margot
                                Zemach. New York: Harcourt Brace Jovanovich.

Materials:

        2 sets of cards each numbered 1-5 (more cards doubled- if more children)

Procedure:

1.   Have children find their number match - for example 1 and 1, 2 and 2, etc.
2.   Have children, in each pair, face each other
3.   Children decide, in each pair, who will be the mirror
4.   Child who is the mirror does various actions
5.   Partner, who is the reflection of the mirror, must copy everything the
        mirror does.

Suggestion to Broaden Cultural Awareness:

It is important for children to develop a strong sense of who they are. These activities provide an indication of how the mirror portrays one's physical characteristics. Children need to learn, however, that inner beauty is as important as the beauty we see in the mirror.

Have the children find out from their parents how their names originated and what it means. Also, have them find out why that name was chosen for them. Have them write down the information and share what they have with the class. On the class bulletin board put up the descriptions under the heading: *We Are Special!*

Collect a variety of books that deal with different cultures. Take to the classroom and share them with the children. Allow the children the opportunity to look through the books. After the children have had a chance to become familiar with the content of the books, have them choose a culture of interest to them then have them research the culture. They should get information about children in that culture. Now have them put their names in a jar and pick a name. Each child will then interview the child chosen on the culture selected. Provide guidance by having children get specific information such as types of names of children, age at which children begin school and at least one type of game children in that culture play.

Activity: *Synonyms*

Skill: Figure-ground (locating words among random letters)
                                   Recognizing words that express similar meaning
                                   Matching words that have similar meaning

Age/Grade Level: 7-10 Years

Book that can be used
with this project: Gilmore, R. (1994). *Lights for Gita.* Illus: Alice Priestly.
                                   Gardner, Maine: Tilbury house Publishers

On the following page is a list of words from the above story. In the section marked "Across" and "Down" are words with similar meaning. From the list, find the words with similar meaning and write them in the grid.

Check your answer in the completed grid.

Title: *Lights for Gita*

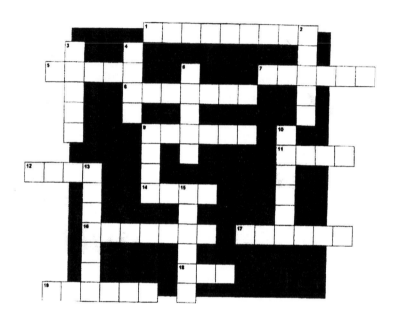

PULL, WHISPER, GLOOM, GLOW, GLARE, SLOW, SPLASH, BLINK,
STARTLE, UPWARD, SUDDEN, TWIST, WISP, IMPATIENT, SMOOTH,
BURROW, JERK, SOB, QUIVER, REFLECT

Definitions: *Lights for Gita*

Across	**Down**
1) restless	2) bend
5) sparkle	3) twinkle
7) shake	4) yank
8) cast back	6) darkness
9) level	9) unhurried
11) tug	10) above
12) shine	13) hushed tones
14) clump	15) splatter
16) astonish	
17) abrupt	
18) cry	
19) retreat	

Answer Key: *Lights for Gita*

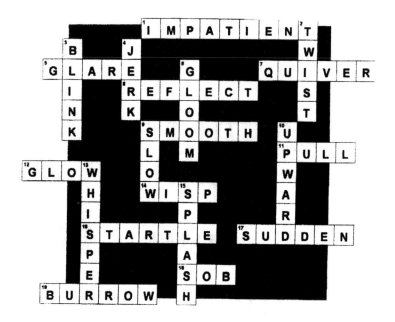

PULL, WHISPER, GLOOM, GLOW, GLARE, SLOW, SPLASH, BLINK,
STARTLE, UPWARD, SUDDEN, TWIST, WISP, IMPATIENT, SMOOTH,
BURROW, JERK, SOB, QUIVER, REFLECT

Title: *Lights for Gita*

Suggestion to Broaden Cultural Awareness:

Different cultures celebrate different holidays and these are celebrated in different ways. There are religious and traditional holidays. In this story, the Hindu festival, Divali, is celebrated with lights. Have children research how some other holidays are celebrated, for example, Kwanzaa, an African American celebration from December 26 to January 1 and Hanukkah, the Jewish Festival of Lights, which lasts for eight days and is usually celebrated in December.

Also have the children research other holiday celebrations. For example, in Mexico the children celebrate Christmas by breaking a suspended *pinata*. In France children place their shoes by the door. *Pere Noel* is expected to come and fill the shoes with gifts.

To assist children in familiarizing themselves with a variety of holidays and the symbol for each, have the children do the following activity. On posterboard list the religious and traditional holidays listed below. On the right beside each holiday, place a small piece of velcro. Write the symbol for each holiday as indicated, on 2"x1 1/2" pieces of poster board. Laminate and put velcro on the back of each. Have the children match each symbol to the holiday.

Easter	Lily
Christmas	Lights (candles, decorated tree)
St. Patrick's Day	Shamrock
Hanukkah	Menorah (with eight candles)
Kwanzaa	Kinara (with seven candles)
Thanksgiving	Turkey
Halloween	Pumpkin
Valentine's Day	Heart (usually red)
Chinese New Year	Dragon
Martin Luther King, Jr. Birthday	Clasped hands (handshake - usually one black and one white)
Dia de los Muertos (Day of the Dead)	Flowers (Marigold or Chrysanthemum)
Children's Day (Japanese)	Carp Kite
Mothers' Day (United States and Canada)	Mother
Canada Day	Fireworks and flag
Independence Day (United States)	Fireworks and flag

Be sure to provide an Answer Key.

Activity: *Using Chopsticks*

Skill: Fine motor development
                                          Eye-hand coordination

Age/Grade Level: 4-8 Years

Book that can be used
with this project: Ashley, B. (1991). *Cleversticks*. Illus: Derk Brazell. New York: Crown Publishers.

Materials:

> Rice balls (put one cup Chinese sticky rice or regular rice, and one cup water to boil on the stove. Steam until rice is soft)
> Chopsticks (one pair for each child).

> * See below for directions for using chopsticks

Procedure:

> Give each child a small bowl with a serving of sticky rice. Have them use the chopsticks to eat the rice.

*Directions For Using Chopsticks:

1. Place one chopstick in the space between the thumb and forefinger (that one remains stationery during use)
2. Place the other chopstick under the end of the thumb and forefinger (as if holding a pencil.
3. Manipulate this stick up and down to pick up rice.

Note: It is a good idea to have children practice picking up small items with the chopsticks before having them try using it to eat.

Suggestion to Broaden Cultural Awareness:

What and how we eat is culturally defined. Chinese, Japanese and a few other cultures use chopsticks to eat. In some other cultures food is mostly eaten with the fingers. In the United States food is usually eaten with a knife and fork (with additional utensils as needed). The British cut the food with the right hand and eat with the fork in the left had. In some other cultures the food is cut with the knife in the right hand and the fork in the left. The knife is then put down and the fork is transferred to the right hand for eating.

Prepare some ethnic foods such as *fou fou* and have children use different utensils, including the fingers, to eat.

Rice is a staple in many cultures. Prepare different dishes with a rice base such as rice pudding and rice porridge for the children to experience.

Activity: *Classroom Family Tree*

Skill: Develop family awareness
                                   Identify family members
                                   Fine motor development
                                   Map skills

Age/Grade Level: 4-10 Years

Book that can be used
with this project: Rylant, C. (1990). *The Relatives Came*. Illus: Stephen
                                   Gammell. New York: Gryphon House.

This activity is to help children understand the concept of family. Even though we are from different background, in the classroom we are a family.

Materials:
    Large cutout of tree for bulletin board
    Leaves made of different colored construction paper (have children choose color)
    Markers and Crayons
    Glitter
    Yarn

Procedure:
1.   Have children write their names on the leaf selected
2.   Have each child take the leaf home to get the additional information
3.   Have the children decorate their leaf with crayons, markers and glitter
4.   When completed, staple leaves to tree to bulletin board.

                      Name: _____

                      Grandparents came from

        1._____   2. _____
        3._____   4. _____

Suggestion to Broaden Cultural Awareness:

Have the children find out from their parents and grandparents their heritage (country of origin). On a map put a tack for places identified in the United States and other countries. Use the yarn to connect the places - to show our interconnectedness.

As an additional activity, put the children's names at each location to show our interconnected with each other and the world.

Invite members from various ethnic communities to visit and talk to the children about their experiences growing up in their culture. If they are first generation Americans then have them describe what it has been for them. Also invite immigrants raising children in this culture. What are some similarities and differences in child rearing practices, parent-child relationships, relationship with siblings.

Ask children from different ethnic communities (particularly children who are immigrants), to share some similarities and differences with regard to life in their country of origin and life in the United States.

Art

Activity:	*Tie Dyeing*
Skill:	Mixing colors Measuring Following directions
Age/Grade Level:	6-10 Years
Books that can be used with this project:	Bestow, E. *Pelle's New Suit*. Illus: Elsa Beskow. New York: Harper and Row Publishers.
	De Paola, T. *Charlie Needs A Cloak*. Illus: Englewood Cliffs, NJ: Prentice Hall.
	Ziefert, H. (1986). *A New Coat For Anna*. Illus: Anita Lobel. New York: Alfred Knopf.

Materials:

White tee shirt or cloth
Dowel rod 1 inch x 12 inches
Twine, fishing line or dental floss (thicker twine works really well)
4 Packages of cold water dye
4 pans of water
4 bottles of alcohol
Paint brushes

Procedure:

1. Place one end of the dowel in the center of the area of the fabric to be dyed
2. Wrap /fold cloth around dowel
3. Tie cloth tightly with string or twine at 3 to 4 inch intervals (width of twine determines undyed area)

4. Put one teaspoon dye to 1 pint of water
5. Add alcohol to each pan
6. Dip dowel in dye or use paintbrush to paint colors on cloth
7. Let dry and then untie

This is a good activity to also mix primary colors to get secondary colors before dying.

Note: *Recycle clothing using tie dye procedure. Tie dye old sheets and use to make headkerchief, etc.*

Activity 2:   *Tie Dyeing With Marbles*

Skill: Abstract position
                          Mixing
                          Measuring

Age/Grade Level: 6-10 Years

Books that can be used
with this project: Bestow, E. *Pelle's New Suit*. Illus: Elsa Beskow. New York: Harper and Row Publishers.

De Paola, T. *Charlie Needs A Cloak*. Illus: Englewood Cliffs, NJ: Prentice Hall.

Ziefert, H. (1986). *A New Coat For Anna*. Illus: Anita Lobel. New York: Alfred Knopf.

Materials:

White fabric
4 Color-packages
4 Bottles of alcohol
Large marble (tah)
String
Paint brushes
4 Pans of water

Procedure:

1. Place the large marble (tah) in middle of cloth (you may use several at two-inch intervals)
2. Tie tightly with string
3. Pour one bottle of food coloring into each bottle of alcohol
4. Add water
5. Dip marble in dye mixture or let children use the brushes to paint above and below string. Children can also use squirt bottles to apply mixture.
6. When dry remove string. Point out unpainted area where the string was tied.

Also show children how to mix primary colors to get secondary colors.

Tie-dyeing with Marbles

Suggestion to Broaden Cultural Awareness:

Discuss clothing such as the dashiki, caftan and kimono with the children. Show them pictures of these clothing and discuss the countries where they are worn and why. Make a simple dashiki, headkerchief, caftan, scarf or kimono out of white cotton fabric for each child. Have them use tie dyeing technique to decorate.

Introduce batik, an Indonesian art of hand painting to the children. Discuss its origin. Use this art (batik), to decorate headkerchiefs, scarves, dashiki, caftan and kimonos and an obi for the children. Have the children compare tie dyeing and batik. Ask them which is their favorite.

Activity: *Dying Eggs*

Skill: Mixing ingredients
                            Following oral directions
                            Dyeing eggs

Age/Grade Level: 5-7 Years

Books that can be used
with this project: Polacco, P. (1988). *Rechenka's Eggs*. Illus: Patricia
                            Polacco. New York: The Putnam Grosset Group.

                            San Souci, R. (1989). *The Talking Eggs: A Folktale From
                            The American South*. Pictures by Jerry Pinkney. New
                            York: Dial Press.

Materials:

                            Eggs
                            ½ cup water
                            1 teaspoon vinegar
                            Liquid food coloring
                            Egg holder
                            Awl or knife (to punch hole)
                            Tissue paper (optional)
                            Cheesecloth (optional)

Procedure:

1.   Clean eggs (if needed)
2.   Boil eggs to harden or use punching implement to punch hole at both ends
      of oval and drain yoke and egg white
3.   Mix ½ cup water with one teaspoon vinegar
4.   Add liquid food coloring
5.   Use egg holder to dip egg in dye. Hold in dye until desired color is
      achieved.

Activity: *Tissue Paper Design on Egg*

Skill: Using scissors
Eye-hand coordination
Fine motor development

Age/Grade Level: 6-10 Years

Books that can be used
with this project: Polacco, P. (1988). *Rechenka's Eggs*. Illus: Patricia
Polacco. New York: The Putnam Grosset Group.

San Souci, R. (1989). *The Talking Eggs: A Folktale
From The American South*. Pictures by Jerry Pinkney.
New York: Dial Press.

Materials:

     Scissors
     Soft tissue paper
     Cheesecloth
     Eggs
     Various colored dyes

Procedure:

1. Have children draw their favorite design - animal, shapes, etc. on soft tissue paper
2. Use cheesecloth to tightly wrap the tissue paper on to the egg
3. Dip in dye
4. When dry remove cloth and tissue paper. Design will remain on the egg.

Activity #2:   *Egg Decorating (Marbleizing)*

Skill: Using tissue paper to create marble effect
                      Fine motor
                      Eye-hand coordination

Age/Grade Level: 5-10 Years

Books that can be used
with this project: Polacco, P. (1988). *Rechenka's Eggs*. Illus: Patricia
                      Polacco. New York: The Putnam Grosset Group.

                      San Souci, R. (1989). *The Talking Eggs: A Folktale
                      From The American South*. Pictures by Jerry Pinkney.
                      New York: Dial Press.

Materials:

      Egg
      Variety of brightly colored tissue paper
      Glue
      Water

Procedure:

1.   Tear tissue in small pieces
2.   Mix glue with water
3.   Use the mixture to apply the different colored pieces of tissue to egg
4.   Wait a few minutes then remove the wet tissue paper
5.   The colors will run into each other creating marbleized effect
6.   Leave to dry

Suggestion to Broaden Cultural Awareness:

Children from most cultures will be familiar with eggs. Have the children do research on animals that lay eggs and where they are laid, for example, in sand, water, trees, etc. The children can also look at pictures and compare the size of eggs, for example, eggs laid by frogs, lizards, ostrich, etc.

In your classroom incubate eggs from a hen or a duck. Children will be fascinated to watch and wait for the eggs to hatch.

The Faberge collection of jeweled eggs is a fascinating collection. The designs are intricate. There are eggs in the shape of crown, rose buds and pine cones. Take in pictures of these eggs and share them with the children.

Children are usually fascinated with the Babushka Dolls (also known as Nesting Dolls and Matrioshkas Dolls). Take one of these into your classroom for the children to observe. Ask the children to find out how did these types of eggs originated and why they are so popular in Russia.

On a chart list (or use Post-It) to indicate the types of egg preparation with which the children are familiar. For example, poached, fried, eggs benedict, french toast and deviled eggs. Which one is the most popular. Graph the result. Children can also research where the preparations originated.

For the benefit of children who may not have experienced a variety of preparations, have an Egg Tasting Party and then use the Post-It to indicate preferences.

Appendix C

List of Books by Diversity Characteristics
(Eight Major Microcultures)

Age

Ackerman, K. (1988). *Song and Dance Man*. New York: Scholastic Inc.

Bayles, C. A. (1972). *Kevin Cloud: Chippawa Boy in the City*. Ill: Reilly & Lee

Boholm-Olsson, E. (1988). *Tuan*. New York: R & S/Farrar.

Brisson, P. (1988). *The Summer My father Was Ten*. Pennsylvania: Boyds Mills Press.

Clifton, L. (1977). *Amifica*. New York: E. P. Dutton.

Clifton, L. (1990). *Everett Anderson's Goodbye*. New York: Gryphon House.

Clifton, L. (1978). *Everett Anderson's Nine Month Long*. NY: Henry Holt & Co.

Clifton, L. (1970). *Some of the Days of Everett Anderson*. New York: Holt, Rinehart & Winston.

Clifton, L. (1973). *The Boy Who Didn't Believe In Spring*. NY: E. P. Dutton.

Daly, N. (1990). *Not So Fast Songololo*. New York: Gryphon House.

Ets, M. (1963). *Gilberto and the Wind*. New York: Viking Press

Fox, M. (1994). *Sophie*. New York: Harcourt Brace & Co.

Greenfield, E. (1988). *Grandpa's Face*. New York: Philomel Books.

Grifalconi, A. (1990). *Darkness and the Butterfly*. NY: Gryphon House.

Joose, B. (1991). *Mama, Do You Love Me*. San Francisco: Chronicle Books.

Kalman, M. (1989). *Sayonara Mrs. Kackleman*. New York: Viking Press.

Keats, E. J. (1971). *Apt. 3*. New York: Macmillan Publishing Co.

Keats, E. J. *The Snowy Day*. New York: Viking Press.

Keats, E. J. (1977). *Whistle For Willie*. New York: Puffin Books.

Keens-Douglas, R. (1996). *Grandpa's Visit*. New York: Annick Press (USA) Ltd.

Little, L. J. & Greenfield, E. (1990). *I Can Do It By Myself*. New York:Gryphon House.

Lowlier, L. (1988). *How to Survive the Third Grade*. New York: Whitman Publishing

McDonald, J. (1988). *The Mail-Order Kid*. New York: Putnam.

Yashima, T. (1953). *The Village Tree*. New York: Viking Press.

Ethnicity

Anno, M. (1986). *All In A Day*. New York: Philomel Books.

Behrens, J. (1983). *Pow Wow: Festivals and Holidays*. Ill: Children's Press.

Bendick, J. (1989). *Egyptian Tombs*. NY: Franklin Watts.

Bruchac, J. & London, J. *(1992). Thirteen Moons On A Turtle's Back: A Native American Year of Moons*. New York: Putnam & Grosset Group.

Cha, D. (1996). *Dia's Story Cloth: The Hmong People's Journey of Freedom*. New York: Lee & Low Books, Inc.

Cherry, L. (1992). *A River Ran Wild: An Environmental History*. New York: Harcourt Brace Jovanovich, Publishers

Clifton, L. (1973). *All Us Come Cross the Water*. NY: Holt, Rinehart & Winston. Eastman, P. (1960). *Are You My Mother?* New York: Random House, Inc. Freedman, R. (1988). *Buffalo Hunt*. New York: Holiday House.

Giovanni, N. (1991). *Spin A Soft Black Song*. New York: Farrar Strauss & Giroux.

Greenfield, E. (1977). *African Dream*. New York: The John Day Company.

Greenfield, E. (1986). *Honey I Love and Other Love Poems*. New York, Harper Trophy.

Greenfield, E. (1988). *Under the Sunday Tree*. New York: Harper & Row.

Hoyt-Goldsmith, D. (1992). *Hoang Anh: A Vietnamese-American Boy*. New York: Holiday House.

Jacobson, P. O. & Kristensen, P. (1986). *A Family in Thailand*. NY: The Bookwright Press

Jenness, A. (1989). *In Two Worlds: A Yup'ik Eskimo Family*. NY: Houghton Mifflin.

Joseph, L. (1990). *Coconut Kind of Day: Island Poems*. New York: Puffin Books.

Kandoian, E. (1989). *Is Anybody Up?*. New York: Putnam Publishing.

Kroll, V. (1995). *Jaha and Jamil Went Down the Hill: An African Mother Goose*. Watertown: MA: Charlesbridge, Publishing.

Levinson, R. (1990). *Our Home is the Sea*. New York: Gryphon House MacLachlan, P. *Through Grandpa's Eyes*

Margolies, B. (1990). *Rehema's Journey: A Visit in Tanzania*. New York: Scholastic, Inc.

Martin, B. & Archambault, J. (1987). *Knots On A Counting Rope*. New York: Scholastic, Inc.

Mitchell, M. (1993). *Uncle Jed's Barbershop*. New York: Scholastic, Inc.

Morimoto, J. (1987). *My Hiroshima*. New York: Puffin Books.

Mosel, A. (1968). *Tikki Tikki Tembo*. New York: Scholastic, Inc.

Munsch, R. (1985). *Thomas's Snowsuit*. Annick Press.

Osofsky, A. (1992). *Dream Catcher*. New York: Orchard Books.

Polacco, P. (1992). *Chicken Sunday*. New York: Scholastic, Inc.

Polacco, P. (1988). *The Keeping Quilt*. New York: Simon & Schuster.

Rylant, C. (1982). *When I Was Young In the Mountains*. New York: E. P. Dutton.

Sandin, J. (1989). *The Long Way Westward*. New York: Harper.

Say, A. (1982). *The Bicycle Man*. Boston: Houghton Mifflin Co.

Say, A. (1993). *Grandfather's Journey*. New York: Scholastic, Inc.

Shannon, T. (1975). *Children In a Changing World: Children of Hong Kong*. Chicago, Ill: Children's Press.

Siebert, D. (1988). *Mojave*. Crowell Publishing.

Sobol, H. L. (1984). *We Don't Look Like Our Mom and Dad*. NY: Coward-McCann, Inc.

Stolz, M. (1988). Zekmet the Stone Carver: A Tale of Ancient Egypt. New York: Harcourt Brace.

Winter, J. (1996). *Josefina*. New York: Harcourt Brace and Co.

Yarbrough, C. (1979). *Cornrows*. New York: The Putnam and Grosset Group.

Exceptionality

Aardema, V. (1984). *Oh, Kojo! How Could You!* New York: Dial Books for Young Readers.

Ashley, B. (1991). *Cleversticks.* New York: Crown Publishers.

Clifton, L. (1980). *My Friend Jacob.* New York: E. P. Dutton.

DeArmond, D. (1988). *The Seal Oil Lamb.* NY: Sierra Club/Little.
Fenner, C. (1978). *Ice Skates.* NY: Scholastic, Inc.

Fleming, C. (1997). *Gabriella's Song.* New York: Atheneum Books for Young Children.

Hamanaka, S. & Ohmi, A. *(1993) In Search of the Spirit: The Living National Treasures of Japan.* New York: Morrow Junior Books.

Hoffman, M. (1987). *Nancy No Size.* Oxford: Franklin Watts.

Keats, E. J. (1969). *Goggles.* New York: Macmillan Publishing Company.

MacLachlan, P. (1980). Through Grandpa's Eyes. NY: Harper Trophy Publishers.

Moskin, M. D. (1971). *Toto.* New York: Coward-McCann& Geoghegan, Inc.

Otsuka, Y. (1981). *Suho and the White Horse.* New York: The Viking Press.

Seger, P. (1986). *Abiyoyo: Based On A South African Lullaby And Folk Story.* New York: Macmillan Publishing Co.

Sisulu, E. B. *The Day Gogo Went To Vote*

Stanley, D. & Vennema, P. (1988). *Shaka: King of the Zulus.* NY: Morrow.

Trease, G. (1989). *A Flight of Angels.* New York: Harper.

Yolen, J. (1982). *The Emperor and the Kite.* NY: William Collins & World Publishing Co.

Walter, M. P. (1980). *Ty's One-Man Band.* New York: Scholastic Inc.

Gender

Barrett, J. D. (1989). *Willie's Not the Hugging Kind*. New York: Harper Trophy.

Bishop, C. & Wiese, K. (1968). *The Five Chinese Brothers*. NY: Coward-McCann, Inc.

Blood, C. & Link, M. *(1976)*. *The Goat In the Rug*. NY: Macmillan Publishing.

Caines, J. (1990). *Just Us Women*. New York: Gryphon House

Clifton, L. (1976). *Everett Anderson's Friend*. NY: Holt, Rinehart & Winston.

Grifalconi, A. (1986). *The Village of Round and Square Houses*. Boston: Little, Brown & Co.

Havill, J. (1989). *Jamaica Tag-Along*. New York: Houghton.

Howard, E. F. (1991). *Aunt Flossie's Hats and Crab Cakes Later*. NY: Scholastic, Inc.

Howard, E. F. (1994). *The Train To Aunt Lulu's*. New York: Aladdin Books.

Johnson, T. (1985). *The Quilt Story*. New York: Scholastic Inc.

Keats, E. J. (1974). *A Letter To Amy*. New York: Harper & Row Publishers.

Keats, E. J. (1966). *Jenny's Hat*. New York: Harper Trophy.

Keats, E. J. *Peter's Chair*

Kismaric, C. (1988). *The Rumor of Pavel and Paali: A Ukranian Folktale*. New York: Harper & Row.

Kroll, V. (1993). *A Carp for Kimiko*. New York: Charlesbridge Publishing.

Polacco, P. (1990). *Just Plain Fancy*. New York: Dell Publishing.

Language

Adoff, A. (1988). *Flamboyan*. New York: Harcourt Brace.

Blue, R. (1971). *I Am Here/Yo Estoy Aqui*. New York: Franklin Watts.

Bond, J. C. (1989). *A Is For Africa*. New York: Watts

Bunting, E. (1994). *A Day's Work*. New York: Clarion Books.

Burke, E. & Garside, A. (1979). *Water In the Gourd and Other Jamaican Folk Stories*. Walton St., Oxford: Oxford University Press.

Feelings, M. (1974). *Jambo Means Hello*. New York: Dial Press.

Feelings, M. (1971). *Moja Means One: A Swahili Counting Book*. N.Y. Dial Press.

Feeney, S. (1980). *A Is For Aloha*. University Press of Hawaii (A Kolowalu Book)

Fife, D. (1971). *Adam's ABC*. New York: Coward McCann & Geoghegan, Inc.

Keats, E. J. (1975). *Louie*. New York: Greenwillow Books.

Owoo, I. N. (1992). *A Is For Africa*. Africa World Press, Inc.

Pak, S. (1999). *Dear Juno*. New York: Puffin Books.

Pinkney, A. (1993). *Seven Candles For Kwanzaa*. New York: Scholastic, Inc.

Porter, A. P. (1991). *Kwanzaa*. Minneapolis: Carolrhoda Books, Inc.

Stanek, M. (1989). *I Speak English For My Mom*. Ill: Albert Whitman Co.

Race

Adler, D. (1989). *Jackie Robinson: He Was the First.* New York: Holiday House.

Adoff, A. (1973). *Black Is Brown Is Tan.* New York: Harper Trophy.

Armstrong, W. H. (1989). *Sounder.* New York: Harper, Row Publishers.

Bradman, T. (1988). *Wait and See.* Oxford: Franklin Watts.

Coleman, E. (1996). *White Socks Only.* Morton Greene, Ill. Albert Whitman & Co.

Coles, R. (1995). *The Story of Ruby Bridges.* New York: Scholastic, Inc.

Cooper, F. (1996). *Mandela.* New York: Philomel Books.

Hamanaka, S. (1994). *All the Colors of the Earth.* NY: Morrow Junior Books.

Hoffman, M. (1990). *Amazing Grace.* New York: Dial Books.

Hoffman, M. (1995). *Boundless Grace: The Sequel to Amazing Grace.* New York: Scholastic, Inc.

Hudson, C. & Ford, B.(1990). *Bright Eyes, Brown Skin.* NJ: Just Us Books

Keens-Douglas, R. (1995). *Freedom Child Of The Sea.* NY: Annick Press.

Lillegard, D. (1990). *My First Martin Luther King Book.* New York: Gryphon House.

Little, L. J. (1988). *Children of Long Ago.* New York: Philomel Books.

McKissack, P. (1989). *Jesse Jackson: A Biography.* New York: Scholastic, Inc.

Miller, W. (1994). *Zora Hurston and the Chinaberry Tree.* Lee & Low Books

Mower, N. (1984). *I Visit My Tutu and Grandma.* Pacifica, Kailua, Hawaii.

Nikola, L. *(1994). Bein' With you This Way.* New York: Lee & Low Books, Inc.

O'Connor, J. (1989). *Jackie Robinson and the Story of All-Black Baseball.* New York: Random House.

Polacco, P. (1994). *Pink and Say.* New York: Philomel Books.

Rosenberg, M. (1986). *Living In two Worlds.* NY: Lothrop, Lee & Shepard Books.

Schroeder, A. (1989). *Ragtime Tumpie.* New York: Joy Street/Little.

Sebestyen, O. (1979). *Words By Heart.* New York: Bantam Books.

Shange, N. (1997). *White Wash.* New York: Walker & Co.

Simon, N. (1990). *Why Am I Different?* New York: Gryphon House.

Sisulu, E. B. (1996). *The Day Gogo Went to Vote.* NY: Little, Brown & Co.

Tabor, N. M. G. (1997). *We Are A Rainbow.* Watertown, MA: Charlesbridge Publishing

Taylor, M. (1987). *The Friendship.* New York. Bantam Books.

Taylor, M. (1987). *The Gold Cadillac.* New York. Bantam Books.

Thompson, M. C. (1990). *Dr. Martin Luther King, Jr.: A Story For Children.* New York: Gryphon House.

Vigna, J. (1992). *Black Like Kyra, White Like Me.* Morton Grove, Ill: Albert Whitman & Co.

Williams, S. A. *(1992). Working Cotton.* New York: Harcourt Brace and Co.

Winter, J. (1988). *Follow the Drinking Gourd.* NY: Alfred A. Knopf.

Religion

Adler, D. (1981). *A Picture Book of Jewish Holidays*. New York: Holiday House.

Delacre, L. (1990). *Las Navidades: Popular Christmas Songs From Latin America*. New York: Scholastic, Inc.

Ehrlich, A. (1989). *The Story of Hanukkah*. N. Y. Dial Books.

Fisher, L. E. (1989). *The Wailing Wall*. New York: Macmillan Publishing.

Gilmore, R. (1994). *Lights For Gita*. Gardner, Maine: Tilbury House Publishers.

Groner, J. & Wikler, M. (1990). *All About Hanukkah*. New York: Gryphon House.

Hayes, S. (1990). *Happy Christmas, Gemma*. New York: Gryphon House.

Kimmel, E. (1989). *Hershel and the Hanukkah Goblins*. NY: Holiday House.

Kimmel, E. (1988). *The Chanukah Guest*. New York: Scholastic Inc.

Manushkin, F. (1997). *The Matzah That Papa Brought Home*. NY: Scholastic, Inc.

Rutland, J. (1981). *Take a Trip to Israel*. London: Franklin Watts.

Say, A.. (1991). *Tree of Cranes*. Boston: Houghton Mifflin Co.

"Trosclair" (Ed. By Howard Jacobs). *(1988). Cajun Night Before Christmas*. Louisiana: Pelican Publishing Co.

Social Class

Alexander, L. (1992). *The Fortune Tellers*. New York: Dutton Children's Books.

Allen, T. B. (1990). *On Granddaddy's Farm*. New York: Gryphon House.

Ambrus, V. (1965). *The Three Poor Tailors*. N. Y. Harcourt, Brace & World Inc.

Anderson, L. (1974). *The Day the Hurricane Happened*. Charles Scribner's Sons.

Bang, M. (1985). *The Paper Crane*. New York: Green Willow Books.

Berry, J. (1988). *A Thief In the Village and Other Stories*. NY: Orchard Watts

Beskow, E. *Pelle's New Suit*. New York: Harper & Row, Publishers.

Brown, M. (1986). *Stone Soup*. New York: Aladdin Books.

Castaneda, O. S. *(1993)*. *Abuela's Weave*. New York: Lee & Low Books, Inc.

Cech, J. (1991). *My Grandmother's Journey*. New York: Aladdin Paperbacks.

Chinn, K. (1995). *Sam and the Lucky Money*. New York: Lee & Low Books.

Climo, S. (1993). *The Korean Cinderella*. New York: Harper Collins.

Cowen-Fletcher, J. (1994). *It Takes A Village*. N. Y. Scholastic, Inc.

de Paola, T. (1973). *Charlie Needs A Cloak*. Englewood, NJ: Prentice Hall, Inc.

Dobrin, A. (1973). *Josephine's Imagination: A Tale of Haiti*. NY: Scholastic, Inc.

Fleishman, P. (1997). *Seedfolks*. New York: Joanna Coulter Books/Harper Trophy

Geraghty, P. (1990). *Over the Steamy Swamp*. New York: Gryphon House.

Gilman, P. (1992). *Something From Nothing*. New York: Scholastic, Inc.

Guthrie, D. (1990). *A Rose For Abby*. New York: Gryphon House.

Havill, J. (1993). *Jamaica and Brianna*. New York: Houghton Mifflin.

Hughes, M. (1993). *A Handful fo Seeds*. New York: Orchard Books.

Isadora, R. (1991). *At the Crossroads*. New York: Scholastic, Inc.

Keats, E. J. (1970). *Hi, Cat!* New York: The Macmillan Co.

Keats, E. J. (1980). *Louie's Search*. NY: Macmillan Publishing.

Keats, E. J. (1981). *Regards to the Man in the Moon*. New York: Macmillan Publishing Company.

Louie, Ai-Ling. (1982). *Yeh-Shen: A Cinderella Story From China*. New York: Philomel Books

Martin, R. (1992). *The Rough-Face Girl: Algonquin Indian Cinderella Story*. New York: Scholastic, Inc.

McVitty, W. (1989). *Ali Baba and the Forty Thieves*. NY: Abrams Inc.

Ness, E. (1963). *Josefina February*. New York: Charles Scribner's Sons.

Oppenheim, J. (1972). *On the Other Side of the River*. N. Y: Franklin Watts, Inc.

Perrault, C. (1954). Cinderella Or The Little Glass Slipper. N.Y. Charles Scribner's Sons.

Pinkney, G. J. (1992). *Back Home*. NY: Dial Books for Young Readers.

Ringgold, F. (1991). *Tar Beach*. New York: Scholastic Inc.

Rosario, I. (1987). *Indalia's Project ABC*. New York: Holt, Rinehart & Winston.

Sonneborn, R. (1990). *Friday Night Is Papa Night*. NY: Gryphon House.

Steptoe, J.(1990). *Mufaro's Beautiful Daughters: An African Tale*. NY: Gryphon House.

Thomas, J. R.(1996).*Lights On the River*. NY: Hyperion Paperbacks for Children.

Rylant, C. (1990). *The Relatives Came*. NY: Gryphon House.

Tsuchiya, Y. (1988). *Faithful Elephants: A True Story of Animals, People and War.* New York: Houghton.

Williams, V. (1982). *A Chair for My Mother.* New York: Scholastic, Inc.

Wyeth, S. D. (1988). *Something Beautiful.* New York: Dragonfly Books.

Ziefert, H. (1986). *A New Coat For Anna.* New York: Alfred A. Knopf.

References

Aaronsohn, E., Carter, C. J. & Howell, M. (1995). Preparing monocultural teachers for a multicultural world: Attitudes toward inner-city schools. *Equity and Excellence in Education*, Vol. 28(1), pp. 5-9.

Abramovitz, S. (Spring, 2000). The Power of performance in multicultural curricula. *Multicultural Education,* pgs, 31-33.

Allen, J., McNeill, E., & Schmidt, V. (1992). Cultural awareness for children. Addison-Wesley Publishing co., Menlo Park, California.

Baker, G. (1994). Planning and organizing for multicultural education. California: Addison-Wesley Publishing Co.

Banks, J. (1990). Approaches to multicultural curriculum reform. *Social Studies Texan*, Vol. 5(3)

Banks, J. (1999). An introduction to multicultural education, second edition. Boston: Allyn and Bacon

Belfer, N. (1972). Designing in batik and tie dye. Massachusetts: Davis Publications, Inc.

Boutte, G. S. (2002). The critical literacy process. Guidelines for examining books. *Childhood Education*, Vol. 78(3), pp. 147-152.

Brown, J. F. (Ed.), (1982). Curriculum planning for young children. National Association for the Education of Young Children, Washington, D. C.

Brown, S.& Kysilka, M. (1994). In search of multicultural and global education in real classrooms. *Journal of Curriculum and Supervision*, Vol. 9(3), pp. 313-316.

Cannella, G. & Reiff, J. (1994). Teacher preparation for diversity. *Equity and Excellence in Education*, Vol. 27(3), pp. 28-33.

Cazden, C. (1992). Revealing and telling: The socialization of attention in learning to read and write. *Educational Psychology: An International Journal of Experimental Educational Psychology*, Vol. 12.

Chinoy, E. & Hewitt, J. P. (1975). Sociological perspective, Third Edition. Random House, N.Y.

Cooney, M. & Akintunde, O. (Winter 1999). Confronting white privilege and the "Color Blind" paradigm in teacher education program. *Multicultural Education*, pp. 9-14.

Cox, C. (1999). Teaching language arts: A student-and-response-centered classroom. Boston: Allyn and Bacon.

Cruz-Janzen, M. (2000). From our readers: Preparing pre-service teacher candidates for leadership in equity. *Equity and Excellence in Education*, Vol. 33(1), pp.94-101.

Derman-Sparks & The ABC Task Force (2000). Anti-Bias Curriculum: Tools for empowering young children. NAEYC, Washington, D. C.

Dworkin, M. (1959). Dewey on education: Selections. Columbia Teachers College, Columbia University, N. Y.

Fong's, Y. L. (1995).Asian parents as partners. *Young Children*, Vol. 50(3), pp. 4-9.

Furman, R. A. (1995). Helping children cope with stress and deal with feelings. *Young Children*, Vol. 50(2), pp.33-41.

Gable, S. (1999). Promote children's literacy with poetry. *Young Children*, Vol. 54(5), pp. 12-15)

Gallavan, N. (1998). Why aren't teachers using effective multicultural education practices? *Equity and Excellence in Education*, Vol. 31(2), pp. 20-27.

Gollnick, D. & Chinn, P. (2002). Multicultural education in a pluralistic society, Sixth Edition. Merrill Prentice Hall, Upper saddle River, N. J.

Goodman, Y. (1986). Children coming to know literacy. In W. H. Teale and E. Sulzby(Eds.), Emergent Literacy Writing and Reading. Norwood, NJ: Ablex.

Havas, E. & Lucas, J. (1994). Modeling Diversity in the Classroom. *Equity and Excellence in Education*, Vol. 27(3), pp. 43-47.

Hiebert, E. & Raphael, T. (1998). Early literacy instruction. Harcourt Brace College Publishers: New York.

Jalongo, M. R. (2000). Early Childhood language arts. Allyn and Bacon, Boston.

Keating, M. W. (1967). (Ed.& Trans.). The Great Didactic. N. Y: Russell and Russell

Kirova, A. (2001). Loneliness in immigrant children: Implications for classroom practice. *Childhood Education*, Vol. 77(5), pp. 260-267.

Klein, H. A. (1995). Urban Appalachian children in Northern schools: A study in diversity. *Young Children*, Vol. 50(3), pp. 10-16.

Kobus, D. (1992). Multicultural/global education: An educational agenda for the rights of the child. *Social Education*, Vol. 56, pp. 224-227.

Litman, M., Anderson, C., Andrican, L., Buria, C. C., Koski, B. & Renton, P. (1999). Curriculum comes from the child. A Head Start family child care program. *Young Children*, Vol. 54(3), pgs 4-9.

Manning, M. (Winter 2000). Understanding diversity, accepting others: Realities and Directions. *Educational Horizons*, pp. 77-79.

Marshall, H. (2001). Cultural influences on the development of self-concept: Updating our thinking. *Young Children*, Vol. 56(6), pp.19-25.

Mason, T. (Summer 1999). Prospective teachers' attitudes toward urban schools: Can they be changed? *Multicultural Education*, pp. 9-13.

Miller, G. & Jacobson, M. (1994). Teaching for global mindedness. *Social Studies and the Young Learner*, Vol. 6, pp. 4-6.

Montecinos, C. (1994). Teachers of color and multiculturalism. *Equity and Excellence in Education,* Vol. 27(3), pp. 35-42.

Morrison, J. W. & Bordere, T. (2001). Supporting biracial children's identity development. *Childhood Education*, Vol. 77(3), pp. 134-138.

Morrow, L. M. (2000). Literacy development in the early years, fourth edition. Allyn and Bacon, Boston.

Piaget, J. & Inhelder, B. (1969). The psychology of the child. Basic Books, N.Y.

Pohan, C. (1996). Preservice teachers' beliefs about diversity: Uncovering factors leading to multicultural responsiveness. *Equity and Excellence in Education,* Vol. 29(3). Pp. 62-69.

Rhoten, L. & Lane, M. (2001). More than the ABCs: The new alphabet books. *Young Children,* Vol. 56(1), pp. 41-45.

Roopnarine, J. & Johnson, J. E. (1993). Approaches to Early Childhood Education, Second Edition. Merrill MacMillan Publishing Company. N. Y.

Salmon, M. & Akaran, S. E. (2001). Enrich your kindergarten program with a cross-cultural connection. *Young Children,* Vol. 56(4), pp. 30-32.

Seefeldt, C. (2001). Social studies for the preschool/primary child, Sixth Edition. Upper Saddle River, N. J.: Merrill/Prentice Hall.

Stephan, B. (1973). Creating with tissue paper. New York: Crown Publishers, Inc.

Teale, W. (1984). Reading to young children. Its significance for literacy development. In H. Goeleman, A. Oberg & F. Smith (Eds). Awakening to literacy. Execeter, N. H.: Heineman Educational Books.

Temple, C., Martinez, M., Yokota, J., & Naylor, A. (2002). Children's books in children's hands. Boston: Allyn & Bacon.

Tomkins, G. E. (1999). Language arts content and teaching strategies. Upper Saddle River, NJ: Merrill-Prentice Hall.

Trostle, S. & Yawkey, T. (1990). Integrated learning activities for young children. Boston: Allyn & Bacon.

Ukpokodu, N. (September 1999). Multiculturalism vs. Globalism. *Social Education,* pp.298-300.

Visions Technology in Education Crossword Companion Deluxe, Grades K-12.

Visions Technology in Education Teacher Resource Companion Deluxe, Grades K-12.

Wadsworth, B. (1996). Piaget's theory of cognitive affective development: Foundations of constructivism, Fifth Edition. Longman Publishers, USA.

Wasik, B. (2001). Teaching the alphabet to young children. *Young Children*, Vol. 56(1), pp. 34-39.

Weber, E. (1984). Ideas influencing early childhood education: A theoretical analysis. Teachers College, Columbia university, New York.

Williams, R. P. & Davis, J. K. (1994). Lead sprightly into literacy. *Young Children*, Vol. 49(4), pp. 37-41

Wittmer, D. S. & Honig, A. S. Encouraging positive social development in young children. *Young Children*, Vol. 49(5), pp. 4-12.

Wortham, S. C. (1998). Early childhood curriculum: developmental bases for learning and teaching, Second Edition. Merrill Prentice Hall. Upper Saddle River, N. J.

Yeo, F. (Fall 1999). The barriers of diversity: Multicultural education and rural schools. Multicultural Education, pp. 2-7.

Index of Authors – List of Books

MELLEN STUDIES IN CHILDREN'S LITERATURE